Roots & Petals

A Memoir

by Mary Sue Gray Love
Lincks Wulfmeyer

Published by Kindle Direct Publishing, Seattle, WA USA
Printed in the United States of America
First edition: August, 2019

First edition
ISBN: 9781686636684
Independently published

Layout: Erika DePalatis
Cover Photo: Mary Sue Wulfmeyer
Cover Design: Erika DePalatis

For inquiries about this book, please contact Sue at:
rootsandpetalsbook@gmail.com

Disclaimer: To the best of our knowledge, the information contained herein, both narrative stories and information/data, is accurate and reliable as of the date of publication; however, we do not assume any liability whatsoever for the accuracy and completeness of the included information.
Mary Sue Wulfmeyer & Caroline DePalatis

To my loving husband
& my family.

Contents

Life Began in a Garden

"Flowers are words which even a baby
may understand."
–Arthur C. Coxe,
English Writer

1

Strength and Graciousness

Snapdragons

One is nearer to God's heart in a garden than any place else on earth.

Walking through our Carmel garden, splashes of brilliant colors envelop me. The sun-kissed roses mesmerize me with their kaleidoscope of hues and fragrances. One of my favorites is aptly named Double Delight. Its creamy center flowing to edges brushed with a deep pink color fills the air with a heavenly aroma.

I look into the dahlias — perfectly formed faces bursting with colors of canary yellows and hot magentas. Their apple green centers prompt me to marvel at their exquisite form. And, as I walk down our brick walk at twilight, the grand fragile tissue-paper-thin Angel's Trumpets explode, bombarding the air with their sweet fragrance. Their hues of majestic golden amber, double antique white, and baby pink, combined with their inviting aroma, transport me into another world.

Our garden, with its rainbow of colors and scents, carries me on memory's wings back to 1937. I was just four years old. I basked with delight in the masses of gaily-colored snapdragons in my grandmother Molly Gray's garden. Those snapdragons swaddled us in colors of vivid magenta, lemon yellow, and deep maroon. They nestled against the side of my grandparent's white vintage 1800s Southern Illinois farm home.

I always looked forward to the occasional visit to my grandparent's rambling home. My loving grandmother radiated joy and laughter. She would use her snapdragons to entertain me. She taught me how to gently pluck off the blossoms from their stalks. With her nimble fingers, she'd show me how to squeeze them so they looked like their mouths were opened wide. To my amazement, those flowers opened up much as if they were singing. I could just imagine them bursting forth in song! Their waves of melodious music filled my ears as I plucked blossom after blossom, filling my flower basket. Thus began my lifelong love of flowers.

My grandmother, a gifted singer, would gently hum her favorite hymns as she accompanied me in her garden. I learned she was in great demand as a soloist at her church, at weddings and at funerals. She allowed my cousin Howard, Jr. and me to play with a beautiful hand-blown glass paperweight, a gift she had received for singing at a wedding. Today it is one of the treasures I have sitting in our glass display cabinet. I will always carry the joy of time spent with her in my heart. I can close my eyes and feel as if it were just yesterday.

How amazed I was, years later, as a new member in the Lewistown Presbyterian church choir, hearing some of my grandmother's favorite melodies: *I Walk In The Garden Alone, Amazing Grace*, and *The Joy Of The Lord Is My Strength*. These treasured hymns of praise brought lightness to my heart, along with visions of brilliant snapdragons exploding all around. Through these, I came to understand the source of Grandma Gray's inner joy. It was her faith in Jesus Christ shining through her singing and mirth. Now I understand why I always felt such peace, joy, and love when visiting them. Their devotion to Jesus filled their home with a compelling glow and warmth. Even as a 4-year-old, I could feel that spirit. Oh, how I yearned to be with them more often!

I never really felt that in my own home growing up. While my mother and father were upright people, they didn't seem to have a heavenly orientation as they raised me. So

The Gray Family.

this made the experiences with my paternal grandparents all the more attractive. I wanted what my grandparents had. Even as a young child I identified with that desire, although I couldn't express it at the time.

My Grandfather and Grandmother Gray, as I affectionately called them, were staunch Methodists. Their lives centered around family, church, and the Passport country store. They were an upstanding family in the tiny farm community of Passport, Illinois, located 120 miles east of St. Louis, Missouri.

This loving home is where my father Robert Wesley Gray and his three siblings grew up. He was the youngest of four born to Benjamin and Marianna Gray. His brother Herbert managed Standard Oil outposts all over the world. An adventurous world traveler, he became my favorite uncle, engaging me with his stories of exotic, faraway lands. This planted a desire in my young heart to travel the world.

My father's second brother, Howard, aspired to become a country doctor; however, scarce finances impeded his dream. To shorten his college course, Uncle Howard chose to major in history. After graduation he taught history at nearby Olney High School.

Grace, my father's only sister, married Clarence Pflaum, a carpenter. She lived out her life as a homemaker and mother. She was a slim, straight-laced, regimented person. Every morning before the sun rose, she would clean her house with vigor. I never found a speck of dust there.

My father, the baby of the family, received the middle name Wesley after Charles Wesley, the founder of the Methodist church. After graduating from Olney High School, he succeeded in working his way through St. Louis University College and Dental School, graduating in the Class of 1931.

Along with raising four children, Ben and Molly Gray farmed their own land. They were also the proud owners of the Passport Country Store. In the 1930s, this store stood at the hub of the community, brimming with every item imaginable needed for home and farm. Bolts of colorful fabric lined the shelves, waiting for seamstresses to create their magic. Huge tubs of seed for spring planting overflowed. There were bins brimming with flour and sugar. On the shelves were spices, herbs, and every imaginable cooking, baking, and canning item to supply all the needs a farmer's wife could have. Heavy, knee-high rubber boots and bib overalls lined the shelves. And, of course, there were many large glass jars, filled with all kinds of yummy and enticing penny candy.

Outside of the store was the ice house. The local ice

truck delivered huge chunks of ice once a week to supply the local needs. My grandfather cut and weighed pieces to sell for everyone's icebox. The icebox was the forerunner of the refrigerator before electricity came to the country.

In those blizzardy and freezing Illinois winters, the store was a popular gathering place for the farmers. They leaned back in large wooden chairs around the pot-bellied stove, propped up their feet in their heavy boots, and soaked up the warmth for body and soul, conversing amongst themselves. What great fun it was for me as a 4-year-old to spend time at the Passport Country Store! It was a magical place for me, a treasure hunt full of excitement and surprise.

This location in Passport, Illinois was chosen by my great-grandfather, Orlando Gray. In 1849, he packed up his family and all their belongings in a covered wagon and headed west from Vermont. Orlando Gray became one of the last homesteaders in Clay County. A generous soul, he donated land to build the Wesley Methodist church. Many years later, my father's brothers and sister donated property for a cemetery next to the church.

My grandfather, Ben Gray, developed Alzheimer's disease in his fifties. That was in the 1920s. Of course, at the time, few people knew what the condition actually was. Grandma Gray was his sole caregiver. Amazingly, she managed to keep their home meticulously clean and singlehandedly took care of their little farm with chickens, cows, and a large vegetable garden. Grandfather Gray sat for hours watching her work. When I came to visit he would ask me over and over again, "What is your name?"

The Wesley Methodist church, land donated by Orlando Gray.

"My name is Mary Sue Gray," I would answer. Minutes later, he'd ask me the same question.

Obsessed with a desire to walk on the country roads, my grandfather would often disappear. So Grandma Gray was constantly on the alert as to his whereabouts. If he happened to leave out the garden gate through the white picket fence framing their property, she was forced to walk, sometimes for miles, in search of him. Years later, I finally understood the secret of her sustained spirit of peace and joy, even in the face of so many heavy burdens and grief. It was her deep faith in Jesus.

I witnessed my father's deep love, concern, and empathy for his family, especially for his mother with all her responsibilities. He wrote her a long letter each week filled with the details of his life, a joy for his mother to receive.

Many years later, my cousin gave me the last letter my father wrote his mother before his death. What a treasured possession it is to me! That letter gave me a much desired, though brief, glimpse into his life. I had so yearned for that! In this particular letter, he mentioned he had come down with a nasty cold. He suspected it was the result of being caught in a snowstorm walking home from his office. Turns out, that particular day was unusually warm for January in Illinois. It was so warm he didn't wear his usual heavy winter overcoat. During his work day the temperature dropped 30 degrees while a snow storm blew in. This weather pattern is typical of Midwest winters, but he was forced to trudge home in the near blizzard conditions that evening.

My father graduated from St. Louis University College and Dental School. He returned home to marry his high school sweetheart, my mother, Carrie Elizabeth Jorgenson. The new Dr. Robert Wesley Gray, D.D.S. and his bride envisioned finding a home and setting up his dental practice. Their desire was to find a small Illinois community in need of a dentist. In their search, they learned of Lewistown, Illinois, a small farming and mining community. With a population of just 2,400, it sat 40 miles from the metropolis of Peoria, Illinois. This town fit their vision perfectly.

Lewistown was a picturesque little community with its stately courthouse and broad Main Street. The oldest town in Fulton County, it was founded by Ossian M. Ross in 1822. Lewistown derived its name from his son, Lewis P. Ross. In 1823, the county commissioner selected Lewistown to be the county seat of the newly created Fulton County.

Mr. Ross' stately mansion graced the town. Mr. Ross had chosen a building site conveniently close to the train station to build his elegant home. Rumors swirled about him being a Northerner, intensely opposed to slavery. Some even thought he harbored escaped slaves as part of the famous underground railroad. The largest cannon made at that time was positioned to point directly at his palatial abode. Until the middle of the twentieth century, it stood as a reminder of the time of the great division between the North and the South. That cannon rested on land that eventually became a part of Lewistown Community High School, where I attended. But while in grade school, we would often play in the yard of the square block site of the then-crumbling Ross mansion. Our imaginations would run wild as we gazed at the imposing boarded-up mound of dirt and building supplies. We could almost picture those slaves, smuggled from the South by train, sneaking into Mr. Ross' mansion under the cover of night via an underground tunnel.

Lewistown historians still speak with awe of the day Abraham Lincoln came to address the citizenry. Some seventy horsemen, wagons and buggies, along with a brass band, escorted him to the portico of the courthouse. On August 17, 1858 at 2:00 p.m., Lincoln impressed the crowd with his stirring tribute to The Declaration of Independence.

Two imposing marble pillars framed the façade of the courthouse where Lincoln stood to address the townspeople. Today you can find them in the Oak Hill cemetery, located on Lewistown's North Main Street. Edgar Lee Masters, author of the well-reputed *Spoon River Anthology,* made this cemetery known worldwide. You will find my mother's large marble headstone in this cemetery. Look for the name Carrie Elizabeth Jorgenson Gray Love. She rests alongside my stepfather, Martin Marion Love, and his ancestors.

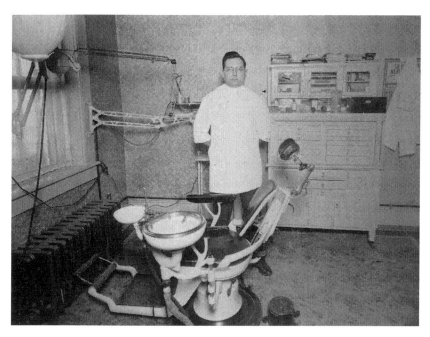

My father, Dr. Robert Wesley Gray, inside his dental office.

Arriving in Lewistown, my mother and father soon found a small apartment with an adjoining office. This was the ideal place for my father's dental office with mother close by to help him. I can just imagine the excitement they must have felt as they hung out their first sign reading *Dr. Robert Wesley Gray, D.D.S.*

The local newspaper, the *Lewistown Daily News,* reported how pleased the community was to have this vibrant young couple living in their midst. My father rapidly became involved in local organizations. The community quickly recognized his integrity and work ethic. He was elected president of the Lewistown Kiwanis Club and the School Board. Mother joined the Lewistown Women's Club and quickly became its president. She also became a member of the Women's Bridge Club.

They soon learned they would become parents. This required a search for a larger place to live. With a bank loan in hand, they purchased their first home on the tree-lined street of South Broadway. They also scraped together funds to purchase a 1932 Ford Coupe. My parents settled down, happily enjoying a life of family and friends.

On a cold, snowy day of December 17, 1932, I entered the world with a lusty scream. They named me Mary Sue Gray, the "Mary" after my grandmother Mary Kimpling

My "Shirley Temple look-alike" phase, next to Lady, the dog next door.

Jorgenson. Behind our home stood a quaint, narrow, solid brick one-room schoolhouse. As a young child playing in our modest fenced backyard, the excited voices of schoolchildren tumbling out of their classroom for recess always fascinated me.

The Fike family lived across the playground in a large two-story brick home. Mrs. Fike was a loving and devoted caregiver for her bed-bound, invalid husband. I came to affectionately refer to her as my "Hoo-Hoo." I gave her this moniker because she would call out to me as I played in my sandbox in our backyard. Her calls sounded like "hoo hoo!"

In spite of caring full-time for Mr. Fike, she always found time to prepare delicious brown bread slathered with peanut butter and cut into tiny squares — just for me. She patiently taught me about the beautiful birds that came to her large feeder outside their kitchen window. During these special visits, I was also allowed to pet "Lady," their beautiful blonde shaggy collie dog. My Hoo-Hoo taught me lessons on how to give loving canine care. Lady would obediently pose for pictures with me. My mother and Irene, Hoo-Hoo's daughter, became best friends. They called this picture they took of me and Lady my "Shirley Temple look-alike pose."

Our home, just a few short blocks from the train station, made it easy to hear the train whistle throughout the day. That whistle, mingled with the *swish-h-h-h-ing* sound of steam as the train pulled into the station, enraptured me. I imagined all the adventure out there if I could only jump aboard that train.

The magnificent town clock atop the county courthouse dominated the entire area. I learned quite young to count by listening to its resonating peals, announcing the time of day throughout the region. These sights and sounds — predictable and reassuring — made our cozy home a true refuge.

Then, one day shortly after Christmas 1936, my world turned upside down. Our whole home jolted from the sudden sharp knock on the door. My startled parents bolted toward the door. Opening it up there stood a telegraph delivery boy. He clutched a yellow envelope in his hand. Trembling, my mother opened it up. "Carrie. Stop. Come home immediately. Stop. Your father is dying of pneumonia. Stop."

Time stood still.

My mother's parents lived 200 miles south of Lewistown. Their home stood way back in the deep-wooded countryside. A huge ice and snow storm had pummeled the region the night before, and our world was blanketed in deep snow and ice. It was dangerous to even walk outside.

In spite of those hazardous conditions, my parents packed up our car and bundled me with blankets piled high. They placed hot bricks, wrapped in paper to hold heat for as long as possible, in the car at our feet. Car heaters were an invention of the future.

My father waved goodbye to us as my mother slowly and cautiously drove away. Tears filled my eyes. I choked up fast. Saying goodbye to Daddy filled my 4-year-old brain with so many questions. I wondered why he wasn't coming

My father, Dr. Robert Gray, my mother, Carrie Jorgenson, and my young self by our car.

with us, how long it was going to take us, and so much more. Years later, I learned he stayed back to attend to his many dental patients and community commitments. And, not knowing the length of our stay with my grandparents, my parents deemed it best for just Mother and me to answer the call to Granddad Jorgenson's bedside.

After a long and arduous trip, we arrived safely at my grandparents' home. My grandmother and mother spent most of the next anxious week at the Olney sanitorium at my Granddad's bedside. Someone always came to care for me. In the 1930s, children were not allowed to make hospital visits.

One tediously long week after our arrival, we received a much-prayed-for miracle. The doctor informed the family, "Marshall Jorgenson is going to live!" We all felt such gratitude and relief. I jumped up and down and clapped my hands for joy when they returned from the hospital and told me the wonderful news.

Suddenly, amidst all our jubilation, there came a loud knock at the door. Startled, my mother opened their front door to see, once again, a telegraph delivery boy with another telegram for her. With a sinking heart and shaking hands, she ripped open the second yellow envelope. It read, "Carrie. Stop. Come home immediately. Stop. Robert's very ill. Stop." It was signed, Dr. Quinones, our family doctor.

Immediately, my Mother started packing. We whizzed as fast as possible back over those 200 miles to Lewistown. The scene that met my eyes as I ran down the hall to my parents' bedroom remains indelibly printed on my mind.

There was my father lying in bed all covered in white sheets, right up to his neck. Question after question whirled through my young head: *Why was my father lying in bed? Why was he covered up with white bedding? Why was that woman standing by his bed all dressed in white? What was Dr. Quinones doing standing beside her all dressed in white too?* Everything was just white, white, white. It was a startling, strange, and scary sight. *What did it all mean?* I stood stock still in great confusion. Mother burst into the room hugging my daddy. She whirled around, full of questions too. Dr. Quinones announced, "Robert has pneumonia and he must go to the hospital immediately."

Three very long weeks later, my Aunt Grace and Uncle Clarence came to the hospital to visit my father. I was also allowed to come into his hospital room even though children were prohibited from entering hospitals. Why was I the only young child in that hospital? It was all very strange and scary. I don't remember what my father said to me. Shortly after, though, my aunt and uncle took me by the hand and slowly started walking out of my daddy's hospital room. Suddenly I realized they were taking me with them, I swiveled my head around in time to look back at my father lying in that hospital bed, my mother standing beside his bed crying. That is another picture indelibly printed on my mind.

Years later it was obvious to me why I was brought to the hospital that day. It was to see my father for the last time in my life. That day, he vanished from my life and his name was not mentioned to me again until many years later.

Fifty years later, a very kind person gave me a copy of the Lewistown High School Yearbook of 1937. It contained the following memorial tribute to my father. This is one of the few treasured glimpses I have of his life.

In Memoriam:

Robert W. Gray died January 23, 1937. At the time of his death, he was a member of the Lewistown School Board, having been elected in April 1936 to serve a three-year term. As a member of the Lewistown School board he contributed a sound understanding of their school issues. His work here, as elsewhere, was not of the showy sort. He was not given to self-aggrandizement. He seemed to be imbued with the idea that there was work to be done and he proceeded to do it, carefully, conscientiously, and industriously. In the short period of time given him, he displayed those qualities necessary for successful leadership. He was conscientious in the acceptance of such leadership, and enthusiastic in his contemplation of his contribution to the advancement of the Lewistown School System. His ready smile and genial, kindly nature, which made friends for him wherever he encountered his fellow men, will be missed by us who knew him well.

The greatest tribute to any man is the simple one, "He will be missed." With Robert Wesley Gray, such a tribute is not empty words. The example of his life will ever remain green in our memories.

In the dead of winter, January 23, 1937, my father stepped from this world to the next. It was a true winter season of our lives. Gone were the bright flowers causing our spirits to soar. No hymns of joy poured forth from those brilliant, velvety snapdragons. They were all buried in the deep snow, and my precious father was buried deep in the ground.

2

Scary Wonder

Bleeding Heart

Raw emotions

Aunt Grace and Uncle Clarence cared for me in their neat, tidy home in Washington, Illinois while my father's two funerals took place. Because my father had a multitude of friends in both Lewistown and Passport, Mother chose to hold funerals at the Methodist churches in both communities. My father was buried in the nearby town of Olney, just 10 miles from his homestead. Today his tombstone — large, cold, and imposing — sits alongside those belonging to his father and mother.

I knew nothing about these sad events. My mother had made sure I didn't. In her anguish, she did not want my lasting memory of my father to be of him lying dead in a coffin. This partly explains the mystery of why no one mentioned him for many years. Even today, my last memory is of him sick in the hospital bed as my aunt and uncle somberly ushered me out of the room.

This sudden tragedy blotted out all signs of spring, which usually conjure in us visions of new life. That year, my mother and I could not see the tiny shimmers of hope so often budding in the springtime. Rather, we were more like swirling dead leaves swept away by streams of melting ice and snow. Our hearts drowned in sorrow as we tried to grasp and cling to the life now taken away from us.

My life had been like the television series "Sesame Street" — safe and happy. Mother's life had been diverse and full of purpose. This tragic, unexpected death of my young father changed our lives forever.

We had been wrapped up in the sights and sounds of Lewistown — so familiar and comforting. My mother choose to sell our cozy white-framed, green-shuttered home on South Broadway. I remember its neatly-kept lawn. How, just six blocks from the train station, the sights and sounds of "my" train would whistle. I thought, "Is it calling out my name?" as it chugged into the station accompanied by its puffing, swishing and hissing sounds. My steam engine always caught my imagination. Now, it was gone. My imagination, full of exciting visions of riding "my" train, had died, too.

My world changed so dramatically. The quaint colors and predictable patterns of life in small-town, early twentieth century mid-America also seemed to be vanishing. Lewistown's stores and businesses lined Main Street with their expansive storefront windows, names emblazoned in triumphant, outsized gold lettering. These storefronts, with their wide variety of merchandise, seemed to be shouting out to passersby, "Come, look what treasures I hold!"

Till now, the magnificent town clock atop the Fulton County Courthouse had dominated our lives. It faithfully tolled out each hour twenty-four times a day. Oh, to think we would never hear its faithful peal again. Or so we thought.

How sad I felt knowing I would never hear my loving Hoo-hoo call to me when she saw me playing in our backyard. This exuberant, secure, and loving world my mother and I inhabited had suddenly become cold and cruel. At 4 years old, all the sights and sounds, the rich colors and patterns of love and security, had shattered to pieces. We felt like treasured crystal suddenly dropped, shattering on a cold, impersonal concrete floor.

Mother sought a new life for us. She informed me

The Fulton County Courthouse.

we would head to St. Louis, Missouri to live with her sister, my Aunt Freda. She had accepted her sister's generous offer to come and live together in her spacious apartment. My mother was very close to her sister Freda and knew it would be a place filled with love and compassion. It seemed to be the perfect place for my mourning mother and me.

Once settled, she intended to seek employment as a seamstress in one of the large department stores. Being a young widow with a 4-year-old child, she was forced to seek employment as soon as possible.

Once again, I exploded with questions. What was an apartment? What was a big city? What would I do while my mother and aunt were at work? This new life we were embarking on made me both scared and full of wonder. We were leaving Lewistown, population 2,400, heading to a metropolitan city, population 13,987 in 1937. Moving to a large, impersonal apartment complex in the big city felt simultaneously adventurous and frightening. Sadness engulfed me. It was almost like a torrent of icy, swollen river water pummeling me, sweeping me away from everything familiar and secure. I wondered what would happen to me.

Mother and I were once again traveling in that frigid 1932 Ford coupe. Sadness hung over us, filling all the nooks and crannies in the car as mother drove us the 150 miles to St. Louis. After another long journey, we arrived at my Aunt Freda's apartment building on Waterman Avenue.

After struggling to find a parking place on the noisy and busy street, my mother gripped my hand tightly as I climbed out of our car. We inched towards an imposing brick apartment building flanked by huge gray concrete lion statues. These sentries guarded the wide, steep steps, leading to a heavy, carved, paneled glass door. My eyes popped with amazement and my heart beat rapidly with wonder, fear, and questions. Suddenly, the door swung open. We entered a colossal marble-floored room.

Help! What was that crashing and clanging sound screeching in my ears? I remember it so well, as if it were yesterday. Across the cavernous room I could see from where that frightening sound emanated. Down the long hall stood a large wire cage. "What is *that* for?" I wondered to myself.

As the door opened, my mother pulled me toward it. "No, no, no—I won't!" I cried inwardly. Then a man emerged — stern, uniformed, wearing white gloves. Immediately I realized he was locking us in the cage! The door crashed shut, the contraption began to jerk us upwards. My stomach felt as if it were dropping right through the floor!

Finally, after what seemed forever, we jerked to a stop. With a loud bang, the locked cage door opened. I escaped! Yet I soon became accustomed to that typical early twentieth-century elevator. It was the only way to my aunt's apartment.

Mother gripped my hand tightly as we walked slowly down that cold marble hallway. Suddenly Mother stopped, looked at the large brass numbers on a door, and pushed a brass button by it. The door burst open, and there was Aunt Freda. She threw her loving arms around us and, with great bear hugs, drew us into her apartment. My loud drum-beating heart was racing in wonder and amazement.

So this was our new home. It proved a menagerie of strange wonders. A kitchen cabinet even opened magically to swallow the garbage! As we unpacked, Mother announced, "Tomorrow you and I will go to the convent."

I really had no idea what she was talking about. My heart skipped a beat.

The next day, Mother once again clutched my hand as we climbed high gray steps leading to yet another imposing, gray-hued building. The doorbell reverberated and a stern-faced woman appeared to usher us in. She was dressed from head to toe in black. A large white collar and white band on her forehead sported a flowing head covering. There was a long chain hanging at her side with something dangling. I soon learned it was a cross. Mother told me she was wearing a "nun's habit." I really had no idea what she meant.

Mother Superior stiffly introduced herself and led us into a compact, austere room. She seated us before a desk. Quickly, she drew out a piece of paper from her desk drawer and handed it to Mother. In a solemn voice she said, "Please fill out this form in detail, Mrs. Gray." Once again, filled with trepidation, I wondered, "What's next?" Mother quickly picked up the paper and started writing.

Soon a young woman with a kind, smiling face appeared. She was dressed like Mother Superior and was introduced to me as Sister Anne. She knelt down, hugged me, gently took my hand, and said, "Come with me." We entered a very large room, and suddenly I felt like Alice in Wonderland. There were books and more books, all kinds of toys, and little figures I learned were puppets. We sat down on colorful but hard wooden chairs. A massive box sitting on a table in front of us caught my attention. The curtains opened and puppets jumped to life. Puppets! They immediately turned my tiny world from fear and wonder to joy and laughter. There was love, kindness, and laughter in this place.

Every day at the convent, naptime was required. Sister Anne checked on us regularly and would see me squirming and tossing, wiggling like a worm caught on hot, dry concrete. I would think to myself, "Why, why can't I sleep like all the children around me?" Sister Anne would gently, lovingly scoop me up in her arms to carry me to the playroom. She alone understood the tempest and turmoil inside of me. She endeavored to fill my life with joy. Later, when I became a Christian, I realized my loving Sister Anne was really Jesus with skin on — just for me.

While comforting love and fun filled my days, my mother was working very hard. She spent grueling hours at her new job, pinning and sewing. Her assignment to do the clothing alterations in the department store of Famous and Barr demanded much out of her.

Six days a week our new life began with a loud alarm clock piercing the early hours. "Time to get up, it's five o'clock," my mother called out to me. An hour later, I found myself in Sister Anne's care, the early morning darkness still wrapping its arms around me. When mother returned, darkness had often already stolen the day.

I barely realized at first how Mother spent long, torturous

hours laboring under a demanding boss who expected absolute perfection. But, eventually, this exhausting six-day work week began to take its toll. After all, my mother was still in mourning. She soon realized this onerous lifestyle was robbing her soul.

One dark night, Mother arrived as usual to pick me up at the convent. Taking me firmly by the hand, she instructed me, "Tell Sister Anne goodbye, as you will not be coming back." Once again, I was silently screaming, "No! no! What's happening?" I was so happy in the convent.

Mother got down on my level and spoke gently. "I am taking you to live in the country where I grew up. You will live with your Granddad and Grandma Jorgenson. I will continue to live in St. Louis with Aunt Freda and keep working."

Once again, there I was—dozens of questions swirling around in my head, sinking into the car, this time bound for the countryside. The 120-mile car ride felt unbearable. Dreariness and heaviness consumed me. I watched the city I had come to call home, a place I now associated with love and understanding, fade into stretches of bleak, barren trees surrounded by black, muddy fields covered with dead sticks and grasses. I wanted to leap right out of that old 1932 Ford Coupe and run as fast as I could right back to the convent and Sister Anne!

My heart ached within me. I failed to notice the fresh green sprouts starting to peek through the mud, or the tight buds about to burst forth on bare branches. The purple crocuses and yellow daffodils just pushing up through the frigid earth seemed a blur. Mother drove on and on through small farm communities tucked between long stretches of no-man's land. Rusty, jagged barbed wire stretched along leaning gray wooden posts boxed in the fields. In some places, cattle huddled together to ward off the cold. It seemed forever before we arrived at the small farm town of Noble, Illinois.

This tiny community had a population of 200 people. There was a grocery store and filling station. My grandparents home was ten miles further. Mother tried to inject some sunshine to the heavy mood. "Mary Sue, we're almost there!"

The road slowly changed from concrete to gravel and then to ruts and mud. We passed many fields and a few farm houses. We drove by a large white frame building labeled Gumble School. "That's the one-room grade school your father and I attended together," my mother uttered in a wistful tone.

Since it was early spring, the country dirt road was nothing but a muddy lane. The car slipped and slid down that sloppy road for a suspenseful mile. Then I saw it. An imposing two-story brick house with immense gray buildings nearby filled the landscape. The surrounding fields seemed to stretch on forever. Mother spoke up, exhausted and melancholic, "We are here. This is your new home."

This house differed from the spacious, rambling white-framed home where Mother grew up, even though it stood on the same property. Parking by the wire fence encircling the ample yard, she grabbed my hand and led me through the wire gate, along the desolate concrete path, and through the back door. Opening the door, there stood my grandparents, Marshall and Mary Jorgenson, waiting for us in the kitchen.

My grandfather, a kindly looking man in heavy overalls, plaid shirt and heavy brogue shoes, stood smiling at us. White hair and an equally white mustache framed his tanned, weathered face. Grandmother, a diminutive woman, cast her sober gaze at me. Mary Jorgenson nee Weidner was one of 12 children born into a family of German descent. She was dressed in her traditional farm garb — a simple, faded, long flowered dress down to ankles covered in heavy flesh-colored cotton stockings. Over that, she donned a worn checkered apron, its square bodice pinned near her shoulders covering her dress. Wispy salt-and-pepper-colored hair pulled back in a bun framed her solemn, weathered face. Her blue eyes examined me quizzically.

As an adult, I now understand the peculiar expression on her face and the inquisitive look in her eyes. I'm sure she was thinking, "How am I, now 60 years old, going to cope with a lively 4-year-old *and* continue my work as a farmer's wife?" After all, this was the 1930s. Farm life was no picnic.

None of us knew at the time, but my mother, Carrie, would soon feel compelled to quit her job in St. Louis in

My grandparents' house in Peoria, Illinois.

My grandparents, Marshall Jorgenson (left) and Mary Jorgenson (right) on their porch. One of their cousins sits between them.

order to be close to me. Mother's sacrificial love for me meant she was returning to the farm, a place of bittersweet memories.

Mother and I stood there, the spacious farm kitchen emanating warmth from its massive cast-iron, wood-burning stove. The fiery glow and sweet aroma of the kitchen itself proved a contrast to the deep sadness hanging over our hearts and minds. Here I was once again, my heart filled with wonder and apprehension while Mother stood trapped in the ashes of her memories. Her cheerless countenance revealed her thoughts, "I never wanted to come back to the farm; all I see are ashes, ashes, ashes."

3

Little Rockets of Hope

Crocus
"Open your Palace Gate," said Spring

My dear mother graduated from Olney High School as Carrie Elizabeth Jorgenson with dreams of enrolling in the St. Louis School of Fashion Design. Her goal was to graduate from the design school at the same time my father would graduate from St. Louis University dental school.

Mother was full of anticipation and trepidation in

presenting this world-expanding plan to her father. His response devastated her. This was the first of a string of her broken dreams. How was anyone to know a second one would soon follow?

Her father's question to her was, "Carrie, do you plan to marry Robert Gray?"

She quickly responded, "Yes."

"In that case," said her father, "You have no need for an education."

She was broken-hearted. Her only choice was to get a job and live at home on the farm. This was the very place from which she wanted to escape.

She landed a job in the nearby town of Olney. Each week driving the short 10 miles to work she dreamed of the day Robert would graduate from dental school. She saved every penny she earned. Every pay day it went into a shoe box kept safely deep in the attic. With great anticipation she looked forward to using it for her trousseau for their wedding.

In the fall of 1929, the surrounding garden and harvested fields trumpeted in the changing seasons. Brilliant orange, yellow and burnished bronze-colored leaves swirled in the air, eventually settling on the browning ground. The leaves layered on the fading green grass resembled Joseph's "coat of many colors" (Genesis 37:3). They blanketed the ground, soon turning a rich dark chocolate hue.

My mother and father's wedding. My father is on the left and my mother's brother, Uncle Orvell, stands to the right of my mother, who sits at center.

Many years later, I would discover what fun it was as these aging leaves crackled and crunched under my feet! It was almost as if the piles of leaves beckoned me to engage. My cousins, who lived just a half-mile away, would often join me to jump and frolic in the leaves. We felt as if we were leaping on a large feather bed mattress.

The year's accumulation of dead tree branches and leaves also served another end: The Jorgenson Farm's annual ritual — burn day. Granddad would wait for a calm, wind-free day to ignite the fire. Striking a match to the dry leaves, sparks and smoke instantly filled the air. Flames leaped and roared as the dead branches caught fire. Spires of smoke wafted through the air, filling our nostrils. Meanwhile, the dead branches and leaves faced their demise. Only ashes remained.

I remember how excited I was when that day came each year while I lived on the farm. With great anticipation, I watched my grandfather light the pile. It seemed as if that dead pile of brush suddenly came to life as it burst into flames. How the flames would roar and leap skyward! It took my breath away.

In October of 1929, my grandfather was waiting for the ideal burn day. Soon a sparkling, calm day arrived. My mother dutifully drove off to work as she did every morning. She worked hard and was saving her money for beautiful china, crystal, and sterling silverware. This would be her trousseau as she anticipated the day she would become Mrs. Robert Wesley Gray.

Her heart and mind was filled with those joyful thoughts one evening as she wearily drove home from her long day's work. Nearing home, dense dust engulfed her car. This particular fall evening, it seemed to be unusually thick. Drawing near her home she suddenly realized it wasn't all dust; it was thick smoke as well. With alarm, she sped on faster towards her home. The scene meeting her anxious eyes was devastating.

Where her majestic, two-story home once stood, all that remained were smoldering ashes! Her parents were thankfully able to escape the blaze. All they could manage to save from their possessions was my grandfather's desk, filled with his financial records, and my grandmother's ornate pink and yellow satin rose bowls.

Bursting into tears, my mother cried out hysterically, "My money, my money! What happened?" This was the money she had so carefully saved. All her earthly possessions and hard-earned money lay in smoldering ruins.

"Daddy, Daddy, what happened?" And then she saw it. The burn pile was reduced to ashes and she knew. It only takes one mighty gust of wind to send the sparks from a roaring fire flying through the air to set a house ablaze. All she could see were ashes and ashes — dreams consumed by an unassailable force. This was but another heartbreak in my mother's young life.

Yet out of those ashes emerged a marriage. Out of those incinerated autumn leaves came a second spring — and a new life filled with spring bouquets of hope and joy.

Out of the ashes of that white two-story framed farmhouse arose a brand new, two-story brick house with central heating and indoor plumbing. My grandparent's home was the first in the area to have such modern conveniences.

No longer was it necessary to prime the sturdy hand pump to release water into the hefty metal kitchen sink. Now we used dainty white porcelain handles marked H and C to pour water into the shiny white porcelain sink. No longer did we have to walk through rain and snow to the outhouse. No longer did my granddad need to dip hot water out of the massive, wood-burning cast-iron stove and carry it to the bathroom sink for his morning shave. Gone were the fireplaces in every room for warmth. Now a simple dial on the wall heated the whole house with one small twist.

In the dining room, a piece of the latest technology greeted us. It was encased in a sizable rectangular wooden box hanging on the wall. This first-edition Alexander Graham Bell telephone had found its way into our lives. It gleamed with two shiny chrome bells, a black earpiece hanging on the right side connected by a rope-like cord, and a black mouthpiece protruding from the front. The crank on the left side was the dial. I learned to dial by grabbing it with my left hand, cranking a full circle for a long call and one half of a circle for a short call. My grandparent's phone number was three longs and one short.

Our phone was on a line with 11 other residences. That meant whenever a phone call came in for one home, it rang in all the others. So phone calls were a community event. Yet because of the newness of the technology, they remained quite rare.

For me, as a 4-year-old, I was thrilled whenever the shrill ring broke the silence. I would run to the phone and pull up a chair. Clambering upon it, I could barely reach high enough to lift the earpiece off its hook. Eagerly, I anticipated hearing my mother's voice coming all the way from St. Louis. Oh, how I loved to hear her voice! I could picture her in their yellow brick apartment building — the one with the imposing sculptured lion guard. As I listened, eleven clicks meant everyone on the party line was listening in. Neighbors for miles around were eager to hear voices from the outside world, and they never missed a call. This was telecommunications in the 1930s in rural America!

Those same ashes of despair stuck in my mother's memory kindled a fire of love in me. The sights and smells of farm life in mid-America conjured adventure and excitement for me. The Jorgenson family farm became my new and cherished home. My life from age 4 to 8 brimmed over with the joy of learning of a new way of life — freedom to absorb the sights, smells, and adventure of farm life.

This was an era of automatically giving your time and talents to your neighbors. Farmers worked together, harvesting the crops, butchering the cows and pigs, breaking in the colts, and shearing the sheep — helping one another all the time. All the while their wives prepared abundant dishes of delicious, piping-hot meals to restore their weary bodies. Through my young eyes, it all appeared so exciting and fun.

And yet, there were moments of anguish. Watching my grandfather leave the house with his gun triggered a huge sadness in my heart. I knew the sound of gunfire meant the butchering of one of my pet cows. I would bury my head in the sofa pillows to try to drown out the sound. Once, as I wandered around on butchering day, I walked into the smoke house. I just started screaming. The head of one of my pet cows was in the large wash tub, its eyes wide open!

Everyone was too busy to pay any attention to my fright and distress. After all, from their perspective, this was just another day on the farm. But for me? It was traumatic.

I wasn't very fond of sheep shearing day either. A farmer or farmhand would grab the sheep to be sheared and roughly flip it over on its back while another man sheared off its heavy woolen coat. The sheep bleated and wailed something awful! I already knew what shy and frightened creatures they were. Hearing their cries made me shudder every time.

But I loved scampering around getting attention from the farmers. One, in particular, stood out. Royal Weidner smiled widely at me with engaging, dancing eyes. His shock of bright red hair also got my attention. I later learned he actually was a distant relative. I remember him so well because he sacrificed his brief rest time after eating to pay extra special attention to me before he returned to an afternoon of hard labor.

I always jumped at the chance to join Granddad when he allowed me to ride with him on Old Case. "Old Case" is what he affectionately called his huge Case tractor. Its gigantic, sharp and shiny spiked wheels meant we bumped and chugged along over the fields. Meanwhile, it puffed out great clouds of charcoal-colored smoke.

Granddad's old Model-T Ford with its hand crank proved yet another trip of joy. How hard he had to crank the handle that he stuck in the front of the car! Finally it would jump and start with a loud jerk, rattling and shaking as we headed off to another unknown adventure.

In the deep winter snow, when it was impossible to traverse those muddy dirt roads by car, we piled into the horse-drawn wagon. My grandmother bundled me up in a heavy wool coat, scarf, hat, mittens, and high boots to keep me warm. How exhilarating it was, perched atop that springboard wagon, seated between my grandfather and grandmother!

Granddad held tightly to those long, strong, oiled leather reins. They attached to large, heavy halters around the horses' necks. He pulled and tapped the harnessed pair of horses all the while calling to them with verbal instructions. Slapping the reins, Granddad bellowed out, "Gee!" This meant, "Go!" The team then lurched forward. We were off for a day visit with neighboring farmers. As we arrived at our destination, my grandfather pulled on the reins and shouted out, "Haw!" Promptly, the horses stopped.

We were spending the day at the Perry Falk home. I learned this was Quilting Bee day. The women gathered their chairs around a long, narrow quilt frame, stitching and chatting together. I played with my few toys under the quilt frame, my own special "fort." Meanwhile, the men discussed all things farming and the current events of the day. My grandfather, owning a radio, told everyone the latest news.

Every evening after we had eaten supper, Granddad would pull his chair close to the massive wooden Philco radio, lean in, and put his ear near the speaker. He was always eager to catch the daily news from around the world. To this day, I can still hear the voice of Gabriel Heater, the news commentator. He always opened his report of the day's news in his deep, resonant voice. "There's good news tonight," he'd proclaim.

These were extraordinary years of freedom for me. I chose whatever I wanted to do while my grandparents labored long hours day in and day out. Some days I would have great discussions with the farm animals. I found the cows were friendly and amusing beasts. They seemed to listen to me with a rather nonchalant attitude as I hung on the fence talking to them. Looking up at me, they would bat their long eyelashes and roll their big, brown eyes, as if to say, "Ok, if you say so." Swishing the flies off their backs, they would chew their cud and occasionally let out a moo. It felt as if they wanted to add something to my statement or, perhaps, were agreeing with me.

The sheep, wooly, soft and timid, would scatter as I came their way. I felt dismay as the whole herd would always run away. Didn't they realize all I wanted to do was be friends with them? How much I wanted to hold their fuzzy little babies!

The pigs with their mud-caked, fat bodies, muddy snouts, and grunts disgusted me. They even scared me at times. I always wondered how those pink, squirmy little piglets I would hold could grow into such undesirable messy beasts as they rooted and wallowed in the mud and dirt.

There were times when I did get lonely and no doubt annoyed my grandmother. That's when she would tell me I could walk one half-mile down the dusty road and visit my cousins for a while. No one ever thought I'd encounter danger, like being hit by a car or approached by a stranger. That little country road barely saw a car once a day traverse it. And that was the car of our faithful mailman!

One particular day when I was around 5 years old, I padded barefoot down the road, enjoying the warm dust squishing up between my toes. I began pondering some strange words Granddad Gray had said at the lunch table. At their house we always folded our hands and bowed our heads as he said grace before we'd eat our meal. This stood in contrast to immediately eating as we sat down with my other grandparents.

Granddad Gray always began his prayer with "Our Father who art in heaven." After thanking God for providing our food, he would end with "In Jesus' Name we pray, Amen!" With these phrases spinning around in my head, I stomped my foot on the dusty road, sending up clouds of swirling particles, and pronounced in a loud voice, "Well, if there is a father in heaven, I really need one!"

Immediately, I felt a voice envelop me. In a warm, loving tone I heard, "You have a Father in heaven and He will always take care of you." It was such a real and intensely personal moment, bathing me in a glowing love and assurance. I hid this expression of God's Presence in my heart with complete belief.

This blessed assurance has given me freedom from fear all of my life. I related this experience to a pastor years later and he told me I had experienced an epiphany, a manifestation of God. Now I know it was the love of Jesus reaching out to a little child with His forever reassuring love. When I learned to read, I found this Scripture in my Bible:

"Jesus placed his hands on the little children and prayed for them. He said, 'Let the little children come to me…for the kingdom of heaven belongs to such as these.'"
—Matthew 19:13-14

Jesus told the disciples desiring to be great heavenly

men in Matthew 18:3, "Unless you become as a little child, you will not enter the kingdom of heaven."

Reading these verses much later, I thought "Yes God, you came to me in such a loving, personal way to show your reality long before I knew what the Bible actually was. In childlike innocence, I could purely and humbly accept your freedom from fear. This has given me peace in many of my worldly trials."

I hid this experience in my heart. Arriving at my cousins' home, I didn't mention my experience on the way there. Living near my Uncle Chandler and Aunt Bessie and three cousins was a thrill, as we were free to play all day together. I would go with Arlene, four years older than I. We'd take Billy, my baby cousin, and climb into the old buggy sitting in the farmyard. We pretended we were traveling all over the world with our baby.

Our summer faded into fall. I was ready for first grade. Arlene and I walked together one mile to Gumble school. All eight grades were in one room. A single row of school desks marked each grade. Our bathrooms were actually outhouses; they stood quite a distance from the school building. Those small white sheds were just large enough for a single seat. We would wash our hands in a bucket of cold water in the "cloak room" inside the school upon return. We also stored our coats, hats, galoshes, and mittens there.

My cousins, Mary Arlene (left), Jack (center), and I.

I loved the early spring, especially the time around Easter. My cousins and I would search through the knee-high green grass in my grandparents' backyard. Brilliant yellow daffodils charmed us as the fresh smell of spring enfolded us. There we'd discover the occasional brightly colored egg, sometimes nestled under the leaves of fragrant Lilies of the Valley. Wonder, amazement, and pure joy filled our hands and hearts as we gathered those fascinating eggs. These eggs were so special to us. They sparked our imaginations and made us feel so grateful, since we had few actual toys.

On the Saturday just preceding Easter, our grandmother, Mary Jorgenson, would brew her special *rabbit tea* on the old cast-iron, wood-burning stove. This stove dominated her kitchen and kept it warm in the frigid winters. Its glowing warmth and comfort lasted well into spring time and it always gave us instant hot water.

This *rabbit tea,* she told us, is a gift for the Easter Bunny. She would very carefully take the deep pan of piping hot tea off the stove, bringing it down to our level so we could see the rich steaming brown chocolatey color and inhale the aromatic scent. The oval, cloth-covered floats in the tea contained the special flavoring and coloring. This was preparation day, not only for the Easter Bunny, but also for the Jorgenson family gathering for their traditional family Easter celebration the next day.

A little later in the afternoon, unnoticed by us, Grandmother removed the dyed eggs from the rabbit tea and quickly hid three warm eggs in the backyard. With a twinkle in her eye, she would call us and announce, "I think I just saw a bunny hopping in the backyard. He must have his days mixed up. Maybe you kids should just go check."

Excitedly, we bounded out the back door. Eagerly we looked for the rabbit by peering into the grass, bushes and flowers. All of a sudden, my cousin Billy screamed, "I found an egg!" Picking it up, his eyes were wide in utter amazement. He squealed, "It's warm, it's warm. Feel it, feel it!" Carefully, in awe and rapt silence, we each held his treasured egg. Carol Jane and I immediately started running around searching for more. Squeals of joy filled the air as we scampered around the yard discovering two more warm eggs. Amazingly, we found just one for each of us. Was it possible that the Easter Bunny knew there were three of us? Do bunny rabbits know how to count? Oh, and imagine how many he will bring us tomorrow!

Easter morning burst forth filled with the gift of anticipation for the Easter egg hunt and the excitement over the traditional gathering of aunts, uncles, and cousins. Aunt Freda was one of my favorites. She arrived by train from St. Louis all decked out in the latest high fashion, with matching shoes, purse, and flamboyant hat.

In her arms, an overflow of "city" gifts triggered our delight. Among those was a colossal box of mouth-watering chocolates, a product of the famous St. Louis Mavrako's Candy Company. To us, Aunt Freda was like a regal queen

My Aunt Freda with my cousins Jack and Arlene.

Our family gatherings. Front Row (left to right): Me, cousin Carol Jane, cousin Billy, Aunt Dot. Back Row: My stepfather Martin, mother Carrie, Granddad Jorgenson, Uncle Arvel, Aunt Bessie, Grandma Mary

and fairy Godmother all wrapped up in one. The precious gifts she gave us made the simple braided clover and daisy princess tiaras we created for ourselves seem paltry and primitive.

Soon the rest of the family arrived, laden with sumptuous food. Such delicious aromas greeted us as we scampered to meet them! With great anticipation, we watched as they placed dish after dish on grandma's large cast iron stove. After what seemed like an eternity to us kids, the long-awaited, magical moment arrived. Someone would announce they had seen bunnies in the yard, and all of us would spill out the door with our Easter baskets. We ran searching through multitudes of brilliant yellow daffodils, fresh grass, and small clumps of fragile and fragrant Lily of the Valley in our grandma's garden. Each of us hoped *we* would be the one to find the most eggs.

Later, there was great feasting as everyone gathered around the large farmhouse dining room table. The Jorgensons were gifted cooks, and we savored every bite. Following our meal, the women gathered in the kitchen to wash and dry the dishes together. Laughter and chatter ensued as the women caught up on each others' lives since the last family gathering at Christmas. Dishes washed, dried, and put away, they retired to the living room, continuing their conversations.

My cousins and I would tumble out the door, joyously yelling and laughing. We were off to play games! Our favorite was always hide-and-seek. Our uncles would saddle up the horses for my older cousins to ride. I looked forward to the day when I, too, would join their ranks.

The finale of that glorious day was playing the Jorgenson traditional family game called "Tag you last." Everyone endeavored to be the last one to tag someone departing. Wonderfully exhausted, we glowed as we felt the overflow of joy, love, family, feasting, comfort, and security. These holiday traditions were so special, especially the Easter celebration of the resurrection of Jesus as we grew to understand the true significance of our joy.

As we fast forward to more current Easter celebrations, our family gatherings continue. Now our excitement is greatly enriched with the understanding of what Maundy Thursday, Good Friday, and Resurrection Sunday mean to us personally. In my growing-up years, the gift of my mother's beautifully created Easter ensembles taught me that the meaning of wearing new Easter clothes exemplified new life in Christ. That is what we receive when we invite Jesus into our hearts as our Lord and Savior. We become new creatures in Christ.

Mother continued her tradition of creating beautiful Easter outfits for my daughters, Jill and Holly. At our 2012 Easter family celebration together, Holly shared her memory of donning a new Easter bonnet each year to compliment her grandmother's new Easter creation.

In more recent times, the Easter bunny began to look like my daughter Jill and husband Jim, who would hide the eggs while the rest of us were at church. The same excited squeals would fill the air as frantic Easter egg hunting among the cousins unfolded. We enjoyed the same feasting,

My daughters, Jill (left) and Holly (center), wearing Easter dresses sewn by their grandmother (right).

as family members caught up on the latest happenings. Now, children and adults alike would play games; no longer was there a need to wash and dry dishes together. At day's end, the same exhausted, overflowing glow filled us with thankfulness for the true Gift of Easter — eternal life through our resurrected Lord Jesus.

In my days living in the country, my cousins and I spent a lot of time playing at Grandma's house. We looked forward to the afternoon, when she would pull a jumbo Hershey's Chocolate tin out from her cabinet. We came to expect something exciting for us was in store, but the anticipation would sometimes almost kill us! Finally, out came her thick, square, homemade cookies. We would savor each mouthful as long as possible, knowing full well it was our one cookie for the day.

The flavor and texture of these cookies, packed with ground black walnuts, raisins, and other heavenly ingredients, remain vibrant in my memory even today, almost 80 years later! Grandma never owned a recipe book. Rather, she had an innate ability to send divine aromas through the air as she created what she called "just plain food." Today, we would call her creations "gourmet dining."

My grandmother's devotion to hard work and excellent food preparation cultivated our taste buds well, giving us all an appreciation for excellent fare and flavor throughout our lives. This diminutive woman was truly the Julia Child of her era. We were blessed not only by our grandmother's cooking, but also by the heritage she passed on to her children.

Grandmother would sit in her kitchen chair, flat black iron in her lap, cracking hard-shelled black walnuts and gleaning chunks of large, luscious, black nutmeats for her signature cookies. I wonder if she ever realized the special gifts of character, self-control, and self-discipline she taught us with her picture of humbleness, hard work, and her sumptuous signature cookies.

My Mother tried to capture this cookie magic in written form so the family could treasure it for years to come. Here is the fruit of her effort:

Grandmother Jorgenson's Signature Cookie Recipe

2 cups sugar
1 cup butter
2 eggs, beaten
1 cup sour milk or buttermilk
4 cups flour
1 tsp. baking soda
3 tsp. baking powder
1 tsp. nutmeg
1 tsp vanilla
1 cup raisins
1 cup black walnuts (or nuts of your choice)

Cream the butter and sugar together. Add eggs and vanilla. Sift dry ingredients and add, alternating with milk. Grind nuts and raisins together and add to above with nutmeg. Roll out, adding flour as needed. Bake at 375 degrees until light brown.

With the passing of Easter, signs of hope for new life began to emerge out of the earth. The first tiny, fragile crocuses determined to push their colorful heads — in shades of blue, white, and gold — through the snow. Their arrival announced new life would come to that frigid, stark Midwest winter scene.

Those harbingers of spring, rising out of the dead of winter each year, remind us once again there will be splashes of color and joy in the gardens of our lives from our steadfast God, the source of all new life. He created and set in motion our earth's cycle at the beginning of time. The fragile crocuses are just one of multitudes of reminders of the Hope we can claim in all of our life circumstances, no matter how bleak they may seem to us at the time.

4

Sweet Victory

Daffodils
New Beginnings – Rebirth

There I sat in the fall of 1939 on my grandparent's back porch, musing and munching on one of my grandmother's lip-smacking cookies. *Why had my Mother left for awhile without telling me where she was going or how long she would be gone?* It wasn't long before the events troubling me began to become crystal clear.

A strange man came to visit her. The two of them spent a lot of time together. Mother seemed like a different person. It shocked me to see her all dressed up in new riding pants, with knee-high shiny laced leather boots and a leather hat. My cousin Arlene told me that she was wearing the latest fashion style for hunting. Mother was the consummate fashion devotee. It was strange and unsettling seeing the two of them walk out the door, each carrying a gun.

I didn't like what I saw happening, but no one seemed concerned about what was occurring in my life except the kids at school. When that strange car drove by the school, they would snicker, taunt and tease me. *"Your Mother has a boyfriend, your Mother has a boyfriend!"* came the chants. I felt alienated, hurt, and troubled.

My cousin Arlene patiently listened to me express my frustration on our mile-long walk to and from school. I cried out to her, "Arlene, you know what's going to happen! Those two are going to go off and get married. Then they're going to make me live with them, the two of them, *together*." A thick cloud of sadness enveloped me. Just the thought of that happening made me stomp hard on the roadside ice-covered puddles that spring, often crashing through them. I felt caught in a web with no way out.

Just as I had suspected, that's exactly what happened. As I walked into my grandparents' house one day after school, there they stood, side-by-side. Their broad grins and sparkling eyes radiated excitement and joy. My Mother, in a buoyant voice, announced, "Mary Sue, we are married now. This is Martin, your new stepfather!"

There he stood by my beloved mother, a man I barely knew. I gazed at this strange man I would now have to live with. He had a friendly, round face with eyes sparkling when he smiled, but he didn't seem to know how to talk to me. I wondered, "Could it be he sensed my unhappiness and didn't know how to handle it?"

Meanwhile, Mother continued chatting on, oblivious to my reaction.

"We're packing your clothes and we will be on our way to your new home soon!" It was all so horrible to me. I loved my life on the farm! Now I would be leaving all my beloved farm animals, my cousins, and the delicious aroma of the fresh-mown alfalfa behind. Once again, forces outside my control were making me leave a place where I had found great joy. Sadly, dragging my feet, I said good-bye to it all. I climbed slowly into the back seat of the car, a dark cloud hanging over my soul.

My stepfather drove down *my* country road. Mother chatted merrily, "We are going to our new home in Lewistown, Illinois, Mary Sue!" I listened, shocked. *Did I hear her right?* Was I really returning to the very place I thought I would never see again? Incredible! Even so, it gave me no joy. I was too miserable leaving the farm – *my farm* – behind.

After many long hours filled with dread, we finally arrived. There I was, back in the same little town, the one I had been plucked from when barely four years old. Now, four years later, I was moving into a much larger house. My new home on West Milton Avenue was across town from my first home on South Broadway. This house, known as the Saer house after the family who built it, was impressive with stately brick pillars lining its entry.

Soon after moving into my new room, my stepfather came rushing into the house, brimming with excitement. He was clutching a brown-wrapped package tightly in his hand. Setting the bag down on the table, he carefully drew the object out of its wrapping.

"Surprise!" he exclaimed. "This is our brand new Kodak camera." It had a shiny, round cone reflector. He slowly attached it to the top of the camera. Then he inserted a brilliant blue flash bulb, a Sylvania Blue Dot. The bulb itself was an object of amazement to me, coated with a smooth and translucent, azure blue plastic. Martin carefully inserted It into the silver cone and then held the camera up to his face.

As he pressed a button on top of the camera, I thought the blue flashbulb had exploded as it took our picture. The flash was so brilliant it momentarily blinded us; however, the picture I saw of us later was equally brilliant.

This new device made the little black box, known to us as a Brownie Box camera, recede into oblivion. We used to be able to take such clear black-and-white pictures when standing outside in the sun. I discovered the Brownie Box

My stepfather Martin and I—along with our dog, Snooks—at the Saer House.

camera got exiled to the back closet shelf, relegated to a life of obscurity. In a flash, its life changed forever.

In many ways, I felt just like that little Brownie Box camera. In a flash, my life also had changed forever. On April 4, 1940, my mother, Carrie Elizabeth Jorgenson Gray, took Martin Marion Love to be her wedded husband. Martin Marion Love, attorney-at-law, was my new stepfather.

My new step-grandmother and grandfather, Mr. and Mrs. Frances Marion Love, also lived in Lewistown. Quite soon after arriving we were invited for dinner at their home. My mother gave me strict dining instructions before we arrived at the Love's home: "Don't speak unless you are spoken to. Watch your step-grandmother and do exactly as she does at the dinner table. When she picks up her fork or spoon, you do the same. If she raises her drinking glass for a sip, you do the same." This was my introduction to my new step-grandparents.

I was overwhelmed. Here I was, an eight-year-old struggling to learn basic table manners. I was used to having milk and food contests with my granddad's hired hands.

After *very* proper introductions, we entered their dining room. My eyes popped as we were directed to specific seats at their dining room table. The array of dazzling china, crystal, and silver took my breath away. As I was seated, my eyes took in the whole strange, unfamiliar, spectacular scene. Suddenly, I spied tiny, sparkling crystal holders with miniature glass spoons at each setting. I was intrigued. *What in the world was the white stuff they contained?* It looked like sugar or salt. Later, I learned they were crystal salts.

My new step-grandfather stood at the end of the table in formal black dinner jacket attire, with a stiff white shirt and black bow tie finishing his ensemble. Picking up an elegant silver carving knife and fork, he started slicing slabs off a huge piece of meat. I sat there, mesmerized. My stomach was tied in knots. The whole scene was very strange and scary for me.

Oh, how I wanted to escape to my grandma's kitchen. It was imbued with the aroma of all things delicious. The table sported a colorful oilcloth covering. There, my maternal grandfather sat at the end of the table. He was clad in farmer overalls and a plaid shirt. I was allowed to eat whatever and however I wanted.

But now, my four years of roaming free on the farm, doing as I pleased while my grandparents worked from dawn to dusk, were over. Gone were the days of having cows, sheep, pigs, horses and chickens as my closest companions.

I clung ferociously to the memories of hanging on the old gray board fence as I held intelligent conversations with the cows. Gone was the horse I loved to race down the dusty road! I treasured the feel of the wind blowing my hair as I clung to his back. No longer would I have woolly baby lambs to bottle-feed. Pink piglets would no longer squirm and squeal in my hands.

I felt such anguish knowing I would never again walk with my cousin, Arlene, to our one-room schoolhouse. Never again would I sit under sweet Miss Betty, my first and second grade teacher. My cousin Howard, Jr. and I were the only students in the first and second grades at the time. These realizations made me ache with sadness for a life lost.

Mother enrolled me in the McNally grade school, the only elementary school in Lewistown. My misery turned to shock and fear as the principal ushered us into the third grade classroom. Thirty-three students immediately stared at me, their gaze curious and intent.

We met the teacher, Miss Graham, a tall, sober, matronly figure. I sensed she wasn't too happy to have an additional student under her care. Her body language communicated as much, even to an eight-year-old. I soon learned she enforced strict rules. "When the bell rings, rise slowly from your desk, line up in a very straight line, and absolutely no talking!" This proved to be her daily call, words swirling around in my head again and again.

No longer was I walking a mile with my cousin to our one room schoolhouse; now I walked a mile alone to my new school filled with strangers. It was a colossal change for an eight-year-old.

The entire student body of Gumble School, the one-room school-house I attended while living with my grandparents. My cousin, Howard Jr., is the third from the left in the front row. I stand at the rightmost end of the front row, and my cousin Arlene stands behind me.

Many strict rules and expectations flooded my life. "Eat properly: Don't use your fingers to push the peas onto your fork! Sit up straight at the table, dress neatly, and handle everything in the dining room very carefully."

Sitting down to lunch and dinner became a miserable experience. It induced a gnawing perpetual stomachache. Being transplanted from the simple country life in a farming family to the life of professionals in the city felt like going from blissful freedom to bruising formality.

In an instant, my life went from heavenly to horrible. The adults around me expected me to transform immediately into a properly raised young lady. I found myself shuddering at my mother's stern words: "You are now the step-daughter of one of Lewistown's most prominent attorneys-at-law. Soon he'll be a State Attorney for Fulton County. You are also now the step-granddaughter of the former Lewistown Postmaster. He was personally appointed by President McKinley in 1898 and Teddy Roosevelt in 1902 and 1906. He had also served as a top Journalist for the *Chicago Tribune*, the *New York World* and the *St. Louis Globe-Democrat*. So you must behave accordingly, young lady!"

The tomboy in me felt just like Alexander in Judith Viorst's 1987 children's book, *Alexander and the Terrible, Horrible, No Good, Very Bad Day.*

"I went to bed with gum in my mouth and now there's

gum in my hair and when I got out of bed this morning I tripped on my skateboard and by mistake I dropped my sweater in the sink while the water was running and I could tell it was going to be a very terrible, horrible day. I'm going to Australia!"

Lewistown stood in stark contrast to everything I had known, even though I had spent my earliest years there. The granite edifice of the Presbyterian Church, its towering steeple topped by a magnificent cross, stood at the city center. Across from it stood the massive courthouse, itself encompassing an entire city block. A carpet of fresh-cut green grass surrounded the courthouse, and the two-foot-high wall was the perfect height and width for me to run along as fast as I could, with fearless abandon.

Across the street, the dime store enticed me with its abundant affordable wares and tempting candies. Friendly Mr. McGrew, owner of the furniture store next door, often sat in front and regularly chatted with me. "Well, hello young lady! How's everything in your life?" he'd bellow to me.

Around the corner stood offices, my step-father's law office for one. The Lewistown Daily News, and the Lewistown Café, where the local businessmen congregated daily for their 10:00 AM coffee break came next. Then there was Churchill's Men's store, displaying the latest men's fashions of 1941 in their massive store window.

Isted's Drugstore nearby yielded my favorite vanilla and red raspberry ice cream cone for a mere nickel. I eagerly gobbled up the generous scoop sitting atop the waffle cone, not just because it was so yummy, but also to see if the tiny, wadded-up paper in its pointed bottom read, "One free ice

Isted's Drugs in Lewistown.

Standing on the steps of Saer House.

cream cone!" Those were happier moments.

Just six blocks away at the edge of town, past the enormous brick Methodist church, the drab county jail, and three blocks of tree-lined streets following, sat my new home.

The Saer House stood high atop a hill, surrounded by acres of trees and grass. Walking down the long concrete drive, elm trees standing sentinel on both sides, to this grand two-story brick house, one arrived at the expansive front porch. The heavy, inlaid beveled glass door seemed a bulwark against all the invaders of the outside world. But a crank of the brass-embossed doorbell to the right set off a clanging bell to announce someone's arrival.

A vast expanse of verdant lawn surrounded my new home on every side. In the back, a sprawling vegetable garden, a barn housing a few chickens, ducks, and a milk cow gave me a semblance of the peaceful rural life I had left behind. Added to this were acres of grazing land, complete with a steep sloping hill.

This hill proved perfect for summer roaming and winter sledding! And a treasure – a babbling brook – flowed at the bottom of the hill! In winter; this tiny waterway gave us an exciting boost as we flew over its frozen surface, becoming airborne on our sleds. We'd have given an arm and a leg for a t-bar ski lift to get us back up the hill.

In the 1940's, roaming free in our small community remained remarkably safe. The town clock served as my alarm, clanging out the hour, informing me when Mother expected me home. I'd often go out and shop for my mother, or stop by to see my new father at his imposing Martin M. Love, Attorney-at-Law office, or gaze longingly at the enticing goods displayed in the downtown shop windows.

On many excursions, people would stop me and ask, "Aren't you Mary Sue Gray, the daughter of Dr. Robert Gray?" When I nodded or said, "Yes," they would tell me how much they admired him. "Your father was so dedicated…," "He was such a generous man, so sensitive to our needs," I would hear from the various passersby.

Apparently, my father had always assured them he would take care of their teeth whether they could pay or not. In those depression years, he always gave to those in need, even down to his last dollar when the banks closed. These frequent incidents made my young heart sad as I struggled to accept my new father and lifestyle.

In later years I was very grateful for these encounters. They proved to be golden strands of thread, woven into an ever-evolving tapestry of understanding who my father really was.

The upstairs quarters in our new home were spacious.

HooHoo, the same loving woman who called to me as I played in our yard when my father was alive, now lived there with her daughter, Irene Fike. Because there were two separated spaces, another tenant, Dr. Don Dickson, resided there as well.

Dr. Don was a second-generation archeologist. He was continuing a dig started by his father when he discovered Indian burial grounds on his farm. Dr. Don was developing the Dickson Mounds to display and teach the public about the Mississippian Indian culture on his father's farm. I began to spend many delightful hours at the Dickson Mounds learning about these Indians.

He was an engaging teacher! I found it fascinating to learn about the multitudes of Indian skeletons there, displayed with their relics so carefully unearthed and preserved. Dr. Don dedicated his life to this work. Today the site is a nationally acclaimed Illinois State park.

Irene, Dr. Don, and Hoo-Hoo became part of my little family. They were some of God's angels helping me adjust

Dr. Don Dickson, archeologist (left), with my daughter Jill (center) and myself (right).

to my new life. Hoo-Hoo was now hoo-hooing to me down the stairs, not across the yard. She would create one of her delicious peanut butter sandwiches, and I'd run upstairs to gobble it up. She filled many of my lonely hours with fun. We'd play Five Hundred Rummy and other card games together, and created and painted plaster-of-Paris molded figures together.

Life in this cozy, bucolic Illinois town at the start of the 1940s was free and wholesome. My playmates Dave Boyd and Keith Hyzer lived across the street from my new home. We had great fun freely roaming the countryside or making lead soldiers in Keith's basement. Dave owned an extensive electric train set we enjoyed engineering together.

Once, I even persuaded Dave to play dolls with me. We were having great fun together when Keith suddenly appeared. He started laughing and in his most intimidating voice said, "Dave, you're playing with girls' dolls." Caught, Dave turned deep red as Keith teased him mercilessly. Sadly, after that moment, I couldn't persuade Dave to play dolls with me again, no matter how hard I tried.

Learning to roller-skate filled many of my lonely hours with much enjoyment. I could skate all over town, no matter the surface. *Clickity clack, clickity clack* I went over the brick sections of the sidewalks, often spared from a fall as I sped onto the concrete section.

My favorite skating spot was the steep hill past Edgar Lee Master's home. I imagined him sitting in his second-story turret room, spilling out the prose of his famous book, *Spoon River Anthology*. I careened down the steep hill, betting no car would come to the crossing halfway down as I zoomed past. While I was spared any run-in with a car, one day I slammed straight into a swarm of yellow jackets. Boy did I make them angry, and in defense at least a dozen let their stingers rip. Oh, how excruciatingly painful my next hours and days became!

My mother and stepfather seemed to be in a perpetual honeymoon, absorbed by and delighting in one another. I was glad to see my mother so happy, but they seemed oblivious to the dark clouds swirling around me.

One Sunday morning, my stepfather announced, "This morning I am taking you to Sunday school at the First Presbyterian church of Lewistown!" He dropped me off and left. I wondered why I had to go there when neither he nor my mother went to church. But I was afraid to disobey him.

With my heart pounding, I pulled wide the massive door to the Sunday school area of the church and went inside. A warm woman introduced herself to me.

"I'm Miss Strode, and I lead the third grade Sunday school class. What's your name?" she inquired. After I told her, we realized she would be my teacher that day. In the class, I met some friendly, welcoming third graders. They were so different from the kids who taunted and teased me about being a country girl at Lewistown McNally grade

The First Presbyterian Church of Lewistown.

school.

As third graders in the Presbyterian Church, we learned how to memorize the names of the 66 books of the Bible as well as the *Twenty-Third Psalm*. If we met these two requirements, we would receive a brand new Bible at the end of the year. I very much wanted to please Miss Strode and receive a Bible, a book of my very own.

Memorizing the *Twenty-Third Psalm*, I made a great discovery. The first words of this psalm, *"The Lord is my Shepherd."* Immediately it brought to mind the picture of my own grandfather caring for his sheep. He would lovingly and carefully carry the fragile newborn lambs into the warm house to save them when they were born on cold, windy days in the early spring. *Was the Lord like my grandfather?* I wondered.

The psalm continues, *"I shall not want."* I wondered, am I not to yearn to be back with my grandparents? Next it said, *"He makes me lie down in green pastures."* Oh, how I used to blissfully lie in the green grass and smell its dewy freshness on the farm! *"He leads me beside still waters."* What joy I had experienced as I wandered by the quiet pond in the field. *"He restores my soul."* Questions whizzed through my head. *"Will the Lord restore it all?"* I wondered. *"How could he do that by restoring my soul? What did it all mean?"*

Miss Strode, being sensitive to my questions about my soul, drew a word picture for me. "Imagine I'm holding a whole piece of candy. Let's break it in two. Now we have two pieces. One is your body and one is your soul. Your soul is your life, your feelings, your thoughts and actions."

"Oh, then the Lord can change my feelings, thoughts and actions?" What a comforting thought! My feelings, thoughts and actions could be changed from the darkness I felt into warm, welcoming light. Psalm 23 gave me such a comforting mental picture of Love. I began to understand how Jesus had made a promise to restore my aching heart and guide me in His direction for my life.

And there was more! *"Even though I walk in the shadow of death."* I already knew the upheaval death causes. *"I will fear no evil."* This statement added more understanding to my personal experience walking down that dusty farm road. It told me to fear no evil *because* God is with me and will comfort me. Not only that, but the psalm told me *"my cup [would] overflow [and] surely goodness and love [would] follow me all the days of my life."*

And then... *"I [would] dwell in the house of the Lord forever!"* I felt just as if huge loving arms enfolded me. Nestling in that comforting cocoon of love and protection, I embraced those promises. Those promises were for me! I clung to Psalm 23 and those life-fulfilling promises as I journeyed along the road ahead and throughout my life.

Some may wonder why I accepted, believed and trusted these promises of God at the age of nine, or even if a nine-year-old's experience could remain relevant for an adult.

But I recalled the experience I had on that dusty road leading to my grandparents' home one day as a five-year-old when God had tenderly reassured me He was going to take care of me. At the time, I had never been to Sunday school. I didn't know about God, but I knew I had experienced a powerful and gripping moment. Although I didn't place my full faith in Him then, this nine-year-old decision sprung from those precious seeds planted at that time.

Now, as I have learned who God is, I realized *He* had been the one reaching out to a confused, lonely, and hurting five-year-old. I was struck how the blessed assurance I had felt then came to life through the very words I held in my hand.

Light bulbs popped in my head and music filled my soul. Once again, I felt like a new person. My earliest memory of music was Grandma Gray's humming and singing of her beloved hymns while we picked bouquets of rainbow-colored snapdragons in her garden. As I think now of those velvety soft blossoms filling her yard, I realized how they symbolized the commitment my paternal grandparents exhibited to God and His Word. I remember the peace and harmony I felt whenever I was with them. They possessed an unusual serenity in the tragedy of my father's death. So much so, I could pick it up even as a five-year-old!

Music and flowers continued to surround me. I was in a strange new home feeling lonely and downtrodden. My new step-grandmother made every effort to entertain me. We would "play" in the garden, where towering stocks adorned with pink, mauve, and red ruffled hollyhocks grew.

Picking the hollyhock blossoms off their sturdy stems, she taught me how to create dainty hollyhock dolls. The ruffled blossoms looked like billowing gowns. I could insert the buds to give them heads. I spent many hours under the craggy old buckeye tree next to my new home creating hollyhock dolls while imagining a happier time. I could picture in my mind my hollyhock dancing dolls whirling gaily around in a vast ballroom.

I was sitting under the buckeye tree one day creating dozens of hollyhock dolls when my stepfather burst out of the front door. In an excited voice, he exclaimed, "Mary Sue, look what's coming, and it's just for you!"

Jolted out of my imaginary world of whirling hollyhock dolls, I looked in the direction he was pointing. I gasped. A large moving van backed slowly up the long driveway. It stopped in front of my new home. Two men greeted my step-father and proceeded to remove a gigantic, heavy box.

In my wildest imagination, I hadn't a clue as to what they were unwrapping. My stepfather's face lit up with delight. Before our eyes, a sparkling new spinet piano emerged. The moving men quickly and carefully set it in our living room along with its own chair. One turned to me, saying, "Here you are, little lady! Come on and have a seat."

In awe and amazement – as if in a dream – I gingerly slid onto the chair. I stared at the array of ivory and black keys. The name *Acrosonic* was emblazoned in shiny gold script above them. *Could this beautiful piano be just for me?*

While I remained in shock and utter disbelief, my stepfather, filled with excitement, exclaimed, "Before you know it, Mary Sue, you will be playing beautiful music on your new piano!" He paused, then went on. "Next week you will receive your very first piano lesson. Mrs. Quinones, our doctor's wife and a gifted pianist, will be your teacher."

At my very first lesson, Mrs. Quinones dispensed more rules. She expected her students to faithfully practice one hour a day, seven days a week. She was a perfectionist. At my weekly piano lessons, she stood behind me, rapping out the beat of the music on my shoulder. Each year she required her students to memorize ten pieces of music. This was in preparation for her yearly recital production. These were formal events. Each student received lovely floral bouquets at the end of the program. It was a show of appreciation for our long hours of hard work.

In time, Mozart, Bach, Beethoven, Vivaldi, Handel and Rimsky-Korsakov flowed through my fingers onto those ivory keys. I began to play with assurance. The word *Acrosonic* always stared out at me. That word was the first thing my eyes lit upon as I sat down to practice. Yet the question continually filled my mind: *What does it mean?*

One particular day, as I was using Webster's Dictionary for my homework, I could hardly believe my eyes. There it was – *Acrosonic!* I had found it! It leapt off the page and solved my mystery. At last, my insatiable desire to know its meaning was fulfilled.

According to Webster's, *acrosonic* is derived from two words. The first part, *acronoica,* means a vesper time or evensong, often called evening prayer. And the second is *acrophony*. This is the Semitic writing of a shepherd's crook used to represent sound.

The depth of this word and its connection to the Christian faith I came to realize as I grew in my faith in Jesus. For that same shepherd's crook also *happens* to symbolize Jesus Christ's love for mankind. Our Great Shepherd used his crooked staff to save his lost sheep, us. He was unwilling to lose even one of us. We were the very reason He suffered excruciating death hanging on the cross.

This is a quote from Roy Lessin, the co-founder of the Day Spring Publishing Company: *"From the moment your life began, you had a Father in heaven who wanted you to know His heart and His incredible love for you and me,"* a Father who would even use his crooked staff to draw me back into His fold. Suddenly, I understood the reason for my burning desire to know the meaning of acrosonic!

During the three years my stepfather, mother and I lived in the Saer house, I discovered a favorite reading place. I loved cozying up in the overstuffed chair by the fireplace, reading adventures of faraway places. Martin was a voracious reader. He took me with him to the library every two weeks as he returned books and checked out new ones. Soon his love of reading spilled over onto me.

One cold winter day as I sat by the fire deeply engrossed in reading about how Eskimos lived in their igloos, my stepfather burst into the house yelling, "The Japanese have bombed Pearl Harbor! Turn on the radio! President Franklin Delano Roosevelt is speaking to the nation." The President's deep, resonating voice boomed, "This is a day that will live in infamy." Shock waves swept throughout our nation, our town, and us. This attack on Pearl Harbor was an event that would swiftly change the course of many lives, including ours.

Martin Marion Love, attorney-at-law and state's attorney for Fulton County, went off to Quonset Point, Rhode Island for Naval Officers' Training School. Two months later he became Lt. JG Martin Marion Love, a commissioned officer in the United States Navy. He was assigned to the Naval Air Station in Corpus Christi, Texas. Off he went to report for duty, and soon Mother and I followed.

Suddenly, my world expanded into the broad horizons of the Gulf of Mexico. The metropolitan city of Corpus Christi, Texas, population of 51,000 in 1942, was a place of vast avenues lined with palm trees and bright lights. Its nickname today is "the sparkling city by the sea." This very humid subtropical climate became our home for the duration of World War II.

My stepfather Martin (center) in uniform during WWII. My mother stands to the left and I stand next to our dog, Snooks, on the right.

My stepfather wanted as little as possible to do with military life. He insisted we live in the city rather than on the naval base military housing. What we now called "home" shrunk to a simple two- bedroom second-floor apartment. But the building was surrounded by a nice yard and a white picket fence. Bougainvillea climbed our outside back stairs, sprinkling a fuchsia carpet on our ascent into our tiny new home. Our landlady, a diminutive woman named Nellie Matthews, reluctantly agreed to rent to a family with a fifth grader. Her neighborhood was devoid of young families with growing children.

Because of where we lived, I had to attend Corpus Christi Public Grade School instead of the naval base school filled with children from around the country. Consequently, I was expected to speak Spanish and know Texas history. As I struggled, the other children labeled me a "damn Yankee." I experienced discrimination to a much greater degree than when I first transitioned from a one-room school into a thirty-two student third grade classroom in Lewistown, Illinois.

Those years proved a struggle for me. They were devoid of music, church, and neighborhood playmates. But, our first Christmas in Corpus Christi, I received a little portable wind-up record player. Music was back in my life. *Somewhere Over the Rainbow, Claire de Lune, Zippity Do-Dah* and patriotic military songs filled our cramped apartment as I constantly wound up my precious miniature record player.

My parents endeavored to inject as much fun as

possible into our daily lives. There were excursions to the sandy beaches at Port Aransas, Texas, and swimming in the Gulf of Mexico. Martin quickly taught me to swim at the officers' club at Corpus Christi Naval Air Station. In the summertime I loved the country club days at the naval officers' club. We went on fascinating and scenic trips to Mexico. The border town of Matamoras was a shopping mecca. There I bought my favorite shoes, Mexican huaraches.

Our longest trip was to Monterrey, Mexico. It was a city surrounded by spectacular mountains and overflowing with flower-filled piazzas and cascading fountains sporting vibrant Mexican tiles. At night, strolling musicians accompanied the señors, señoras and señoritas promenading the streets gaily clad in brilliant Mexican colors. The blossoms of sweet-smelling jasmine perfumed the night air. These moments were the southern culture version of a soothing balm. It brought relief to the heartaches and tough adjustments of war.

After what seemed like an eternity (but, in fact, was just over three years), the much prayed-for news came. The Japanese had surrendered! On the heels of this news came that of the German surrender. World War II was over!

Our world erupted into joyous, grateful, riotous celebration. The people in Corpus Christi and all over the

U.S. poured out onto city streets. Streets filled with sailors grabbing girls and kissing them, tossing their white sailor hats high into the air. Triumphal horns blew nonstop. People cheered, hugging and kissing perfect strangers. We celebrated the victory together, united. We yelled at the top of our lungs as we jumped in wild jubilation. "The war's over. The war's over and we can go home!"

What a moment of thanksgiving and rejoicing! Our soldiers came home to ticker-tape parades, waving American flags, massive crowds of people cheering and shouting appreciation for their sacrifice and victorious return.

Martin immediately announced, "The war is won and our Texas battle is over. We are going home!"

I pleaded, "Oh, can't we stay just six more weeks so I can graduate from eighth grade?"

Awareness that the southern school curriculum was years behind that of the northern schools filled me with dread. How would I ever be able to graduate from 8th grade? I was missing two years of grade school education. That was the ONLY reason I wanted to spend six more weeks in Texas. Martin's response to my pleading was firm. "No, we are returning home as soon as we possibly can."

We packed and packed until we were barely able to squeeze ourselves into our 1941 Ford. We returned to Lewistown with hearts eager to plant our feet once again on the solid soil of middle America. We were no longer aliens in the "foreign" land of Texas. We had won "the battle of Corpus Christi Bay," as Martin had coined it.

Upon arrival, I was in shock at how things – and

especially people – had changed. Those Lewistown friends I so pined away for in Texas now had other friends. I was once again the outsider.

This proved another valuable life lesson for me. I grew to understand the memory of what existed in the past may be different from what the current reality is. Expecting everything to remain the same leads to great disappointment. This hit me like a shocking, painful bee sting. But, much like a bee, it also made honey. The sweet taste of a new life was emerging. And I did graduate in six weeks from the eighth grade.

5

Success

Amaryllis

Harmony with self and others

"Come and sample, come and inhale," I called out to the crowd.

I wanted others to experience and enjoy the exhilarating, sweet aroma of lavender mist as well as the other original scents my daughter Jill had created. I was thrilled to assist her in marketing the organic bath, spa and skin products she had created into a new business, *Absolute Naturals*. That very moment transported me back to my high school years in the late 1940s.

"Come and get it!" I yelled repeatedly above the din of a crowded high school gymnasium. "We've got steaming hotdogs and hamburgers, chocolate chip cookies and potato chips, popcorn and peanuts. Come and get it!" As student council members, we aimed to raise needed funds for the school. The annual basketball tournament in January proved an ideal venue.

Students and parents packed the high school gym. Cheers for Lewistown High School, the Lewistown Indians, and the red and blue, resonated throughout. Friends yelled, cheered, and did everything possible to encourage our team. They were in a hot contest for the Fulton County basketball finals. Ear-piercing cheers rang out as Keith Hyzer, our star athlete, made a perfect basket!!! Two more points lit up on the scoreboard, buzzing loudly.

Then the referees blew their shrill whistles and shouted, "Foul!" – against the other team. Oh, for just two perfect free throws to clinch the game! *Swish* went the first shot, straight through the basketball hoop. Everyone held their breath as silence descended upon the team. The tension proved palpable. *Swish* – and, once again, Keith sent a perfect shot through the basket! The gym reverberated with joyous shouts of, "Victory! Victory!"

Our Lewistown Indians basketball team won! After so many missed baskets and so many disheartening losses, getting to the finals was a miracle in itself. Winning the title filled everyone in that Lewistown High School gymnasium with the glow of sweet success.

The crisp and colorful Midwest fall weather meant a world filled with brilliant oak leaves and acorns carpeting the ground, often crunching under our feet. In spring, blooming dogwood and redbud trees lined the streets, leading the way to the track meets on a field adjacent to our school. To my surprise, the track team unanimously elected me their queen in my junior year. It was a privilege to present our players with their ribbons and trophies.

Winning major roles in both the junior and senior class plays proved a highlight of my time at Lewistown High School. And I loved all the excitement swirling around our Junior-Senior proms, as we turned our gym into a magical place. On those nights, we crowned a king and queen and danced the night away to 1950s tunes. My gifted mother always created formal dresses in the latest styles, prepared just for me. Indeed, much like our basketball team, I was experiencing the sweet encouragement of success for the very first time in my life.

Success and confidence spilled over into my personal life as well. My years of defeat and frustration gradually receded into my memory. Left behind were the taunts of discrimination I had endured while in Texas. I was soaring on eagles' wings above the past.

I eagerly pursued my new high school courses of biology, algebra, and English literature. Self-assurance began to fill my heart. I was elected class secretary and president of student council.

My biology teacher invited me to enter his coaching class for competitive poetry reading. Entering the countywide poetry reading competition gave me mixed feelings. Though dealing with some fear, I also savored the challenge. Turns out I got to experience my first taste of victory, bringing home a medal for my high school. Earning medals in the poetry reading contests ushered in a new confidence to speak before a critical audience of judges. I always found the high school state competitions in music and literature exciting, challenging and, of course, loads of fun.

As a member of our high school chorus, we had the opportunity to sing in the countywide music competition. What a thrill of victory for the 30 of us when we won the top honor for our school! We owed many thanks to the dedication of Mr. Jorgensen, our choral director.

When I was elected student council president, I learned about *Robert's Rules Of Order,* as anyone in leadership had to become familiar with the contents of this tome. This book taught me lessons of proper protocol used for conducting group meetings. It has proven valuable throughout my life. Through this position, I also got to meet with other statewide student council members to enhance our leadership capability.

Yet another great honor for me was my induction into the Quill and Scroll society. The society presented me with a medal signifying I had done outstanding work on our school newspaper, *The Tomahawk*.

Indeed, high school was my first positive school experience, and I reveled in it. I felt like I had been plucked out of a quagmire of clay and given a crown of gold. Like Cinderella, my cinders had changed to gold.

During this time, I discovered new life spiritually as well. I decided to get baptized and become a member of the First Presbyterian Church of Lewistown. The Sunday School superintendent even invited me to teach the kindergarten class. Through this experience, I discovered my joy of teaching young children so eager to learn.

Being invited to sing in the church choir launched me into a season of exhilaration. I love singing to this day! *Amazing Grace* was one of the many uplifting hymns we sang in the choir of the Presbyterian Church. Every Thursday I walked the three short blocks to church for choir practice. On Sunday we arrived early to don our long choir robes with satin scarves to sing in harmony with our director and organist, Mrs. Bowton. On Easter Sunday, we sang the magnificent Handel's *Messiah*. Singing spiritual hymns imbued with deep meaning transported me to the heavens.

Our high school church youth group had fun together studying God's Word. Each summer we attended the all-state Presbyterian summer camp held at Monmouth College in Monmouth, Illinois. My camper friends even elected me Moderator one of those years – something unimaginable to

A portrait taken of me during my junior year of high school.

me. I embraced the position with a spirit of vitality and joy.

At youth camp, we began our day with Bible study, led by wise Presbyterian pastors from around the state of Illinois. Later came time to swim, roller skate, and simply hang out together. After a hearty dinner, we regularly attended Vespers, a quiet time of contemplation. Later, fun-filled games and folk dancing finished off the day. We'd fall into our beds exhausted.

When we returned home from camp, our youth group was given the privilege of writing, organizing, and conducting the Sunday church services every August. This was our pastor's traditional vacation month. Together, we savored this opportunity to share from God's Word like fresh springs arising from our own personal spiritual growth at camp.

It was while attending church camp that I learned one of my favorite songs, *White Coral Bells*. Its lyrics still reverberate in my head today:

"White coral bells upon a slender stalk, lilies of the valley deck my garden walk.
Oh, don't you wish that you could hear them ring? That will happen only when the angels sing."

I felt as if angels were continually singing to my heart throughout my high school years.

Music was very much a part of our family. During family trips to St. Louis, I discovered how exciting light opera was while watching fantastic dance teams and gifted vocalists. Those magical performances of *The Desert Song, The Flower Drum Song,* and *Porgy and Bess,* along with many others, resonate in my heart and mind. I can still picture those performances under the stars on the magnificent stage built for the St. Louis World's Fair of 1904. Today we call it The Muny Opera.

My love of flowers was deepened by visits to the world-famous Missouri Botanical Gardens. The garden's vast profusion of flowers and exotic plants dazzled my senses. I also relished outings to the St. Louis Art Museum and the St. Louis Zoo. All these attractions are located on the grounds of the 1904 World's Fair. Today the name of that area is Forest Park. It was that very place in 1904 where the world's first ice cream cone and hot dog were created. It was also the site for the inspiration of the classic movie, *Meet Me In St. Louis.*

Noticing my heart for singing as well as playing the piano, my parents sought to encourage me however possible. They drove forty miles every week to Peoria, Illinois to take me to voice lessons. I didn't fully realize their sacrifice until I became a parent myself. Thanks to their dedication, I had the experience of singing solo in recitals and local programs. Now I was truly experiencing the joy and thrill of accomplishment.

One summer day, I let out unrestrained shouts of joy as I threw my graduation cap into the sky. Head held high, clutching my diploma, I felt both psychologically and spiritually ready to fulfill my mother's mantra: "Get an education and you can always take care of yourself."

I possessed the quiet inner joy of self-worth and confidence – along with some trepidation – as I faced the unknown world of college. I believed I could get an education and take care of myself.

It was 1950.

I'm astounded to learn now, with the research for this book, how few women in my day actually attended college, much less completed their degree. For me, I always thought it would be a given, namely because of the positive educational influences my immediate family had upon me. My father had been a dentist, necessitating higher education. My stepfather was a lawyer, so he clearly went beyond his first four years of higher education. My mother always talked about going further than high school but was never able to achieve that in her day, even though she yearned to do so. Still, she graduated from high school, an accomplishment many other women at that time couldn't claim.

I would learn later how in the year I graduated from college, less than 5.8% of all female adults in the U.S. held a college degree. (That amount was 8.3% for men.) Looking back, I now realize how rare – and how fortunate – I was. All I can say is how deeply grateful I remain.

Decisions, decisions. What college to attend? What career to choose? My older cousins, Doris and Arlene, were nurses. Like them, I wanted to help people and thought nursing was the career for me. Listening to Arlene's horror stories about working in the emergency room of a large hospital gave me pause, however. Was nursing for me? Surely there was a career helping others I could enjoy more. But what? Oh – I loved music! Since the day my stepfather had surprised me with that fabulous piano, music had helped me soar above the struggles of my growing-up years. Sitting at my piano playing and singing songs like *Trees* filled my heart with hope.

I think that I shall never see a poem lovely as a tree,
A tree whose hungry mouth is pressed
Against the earth's sweet flowing breast;
A tree that looks at God all day
And lifts her leafy arms to pray,
A tree that may in summer wears
A nest of robins in its hair;
Upon whose bosom snow has lain;
And intimately lives with rain.
Poems are made by fools like me
But only God can make a tree.

I claimed that song as a description of my spiritual outlook at the time. The only piano teacher in Lewistown, Mrs. Quinones, had spent years teaching me to play classical music by Bach, Beethoven, and Haydn. We were not allowed to play the popular music of the day. She required her students to memorize ten pieces of music for her yearly recitals. Another student, Maureen Reinhardt, and I played duets together. We even put on an evening ensemble of duet piano music in the Lewistown Methodist church. As I pondered all this, I thought, "That's it – I will major in music!"

Armed with the idea for a college major, I poured over stacks of college catalogs to choose just the right college. It soon became apparent Grinnell College in Grinnell, Iowa was the one best fitting my vision. A highly rated small college, it offered an excellent music program with strong faculty. In the 1950's, if you fulfilled the college requirements in high school with a C or better grade average, you pretty much could chose the college you wanted to attend. Colleges were eager for enrollees.

Off I went in the fall of 1950 to Grinnell. This small Midwestern college had students from all over the world along with many from Chicago, Illinois and St. Louis, Missouri.

My freshman year was filled with new discoveries about the world and about myself. For one, I soon came to realize that I definitely *didn't* have the dedication or talent to become a professional pianist. Being closed up in a soundproof, windowless room just big enough for a piano was claustrophobic and stifling for me. I observed talented musicians – much more talented than I – eagerly enter those practice rooms.

Singing caught my fancy, however. I studied voice with Dr. Hornung. She arranged vocal performances throughout Iowa for her students. These excursions taught us great stage presence and delight in meeting many people. Once again, I enjoyed the opportunity of singing in a church choir, this time in the beautiful Gothic Grinnell chapel on our campus.

And yet another discovery: I found I thoroughly enjoyed research, writing, and extemporaneous speaking. That shouldn't have surprised me as I thought about my summer job between high school and college as a reporter for the *Lewistown Daily News*.

It had always been my plan to start college at a small school and then transfer to a large university. During this first year at Grinnell, I learned it would be best to complete any transfer application to a major university within my first year. Doing this would minimize the loss of credits.

The best friends I made at Grinnell were from St. Louis. They planned to return home and attend Washington University in St. Louis.

I researched this university and learned it was ranked in the top ten universities in the United Stated in 1950. My parents and I met with the Dean of Admissions. We toured the lovely campus filled with impressive brick buildings of Gothic architecture, and we studied their extensive curriculum.

So I applied and received a welcome from my new home for the rest of my college career. I began Year 2 at Washington University in the fall of 1951. Some of my new-found friends nudged me to go through sorority rush. I realized doing so would allow me to connect with people from all over, expanding my world. Along with my best friend Joyce Lewis, I accepted Kappa Kappa Gamma's bid. Through this organization, I learned the great pleasure of being involved in philanthropic projects.

Now, once again, my dilemma of a major was haunting me. I called it my sophomore search year.

Standing in line to sign up for a general liberal arts program, I spied a shorter line. A friend in that line for pre-med students said, "This course is notorious for flunking out students desiring to become doctors."

I wondered to myself if I could pass such a course. Sign up I did, and pass I did! But, for me, my motivation was just the nature of the challenge, not a burning desire to become a doctor.

During that year, I recalled my delight in seeing small, shining faces listen and learn God's Word during my years of leading Sunday School as a high schooler at my church. I delighted in teaching them songs containing Biblical stories and truths, such as *Jonah and The Big Fish* and *We Are Climbing Jacob's Ladder*. At the conclusion of that year, I knew Education would be my major.

Living in a large city appealed to me, so the thought of spending the upcoming summer in Lewistown seemed very boring. I stood in the dimly-lit hallway of the Education building, scanning the glass-encased bulletin board, searching for a summer job. Suddenly, my eyes lit upon a 3x5 card that read:

Wanted: An education student to live in our home
and care for our children,
Signed Mr. and Mrs. Morton D. May.

"Hmmmm, I wonder who they are," I thought to myself. "Maybe my sorority sisters from St. Louis will know. I'll ask them." Their immediate response was, "Call at once and apply for the job!! This is an opportunity of a lifetime." They informed me that Morton D. May was chairman of the board of the May department stores, including the famous May Company of California. The May Company department store in St. Louis was called Famous and Barr. It was the largest and best store in the city.

The elder Mr. May's home was at Number 5 Brentwood Place, just two blocks from the university. As I walked along, his impressive mansion came into view. I slowly stepped across the enclosed brick-pillared drive and approached the massive front door. Glancing at my watch, I thought, "Good, I'm right on time for my appointment with Mrs. May!"

Taking a deep breath for courage, I lifted the heavy brass knocker and waited. The butler formally greeted me and led me through a never-ending entry room hung with massive original paintings. It felt as if I were walking through the St. Louis Art Museum! He escorted me up the long, wide staircase and down another lengthy hall. Stopping at one door, he announced in a thundering voice, "Miss Gray is here for her appointment."

Immediately, a tall woman with a business-like demeanor opened the door. With a slight smile, she invited me in. She motioned for me to be seated, introduced herself, and interviewed me extensively. She told me I would be caring for their two-year-old son, M.J., and Mrs. May's five-year-old twin daughters by a former marriage, Laura and Ann.

My position as governess was to be casual, no uniform required. I was to be a companion, blending in with the family and accompanying them wherever they went. She gave me explicit instructions to never let the children out of my sight. Fear of kidnapping was one of their great concerns.

Mrs. May explained they were currently building their permanent family residence on an adjacent property. Upon completion, I was to live with them. In the meantime, I would continue living in my college dorm. Throughout this lengthy interview she stared intently at me, unwavering. I felt as if she could see right through me. It was jarring.

Finally, with an air of decisiveness, she announced, "Miss Gray, I am offering you this position. I believe you are the person we are looking for." My heart pounded and my head swirled with delight as I responded, "I accept your offer for this summer job!" Inside, my silent voice bellowed within me, "Whoopee!!!" I could spend all summer in St. Louis!

My "summer job" position lasted until I graduated. Those three years were like a Cinderella story in so many ways. I was treated like part of the family. I sat at the dinner table with the family, facing the enormous Picasso painting on the dining room wall, and was served along with them. On my one day off a week, I was allowed to swim and sunbathe by the pool. I was the one who asked the chauffeur to drive the children and myself to their favorite park to play and get ice cream. The butler, cook, housekeeper, ironing lady, chauffeur, and gardener envied me a bit for my swift and secure acceptance into the family. But they tolerated it with good humor, I believe.

Later, the May family allowed me to hold a bridal shower for a dear friend at their home. This time, I was the one giving all the workers instructions for the event. On that day *I* was the one sitting at the head of the table instead of Mrs. May. *I* was the one pushing the servant's bell below the tabletop for the butler when our luncheon was to be served. This special "authority" continued as, from time to time during these three years, I was also allowed to entertain my school friends during the year.

At the May home, there were famous people to meet and entertain, like Arturo Toscanini and influential businessmen from around the United States. There were family summer vacations to places like Bermuda where we lived in a large home overlooking our own private beach.

This summer job, one of my earliest paying jobs, taught me that true riches are in relationships and experiences. Wealthy people have just as many problems and responsibilities as anyone else; in fact, they often have more because of their great wealth.

6

Love Personified

Lilies of the Valley

An autumn crocus' SWEET AROMA growing in deep and difficult places

Rushing across the campus to my final semester of college, I literally ran headlong into a handsome fellow student. My books and papers scattered all over the fresh green grass. He gallantly retrieved them for me. Profusely thanking him, I proceeded on my fast track to class.

"Wait just a minute!" he bellowed. "Can't we at least introduce ourselves and walk together to class?" Calculating the time, I agreed to momentarily slow my pace. After introductions and the usual student small talk of classes, our majors – his Architecture, and mine Education – we arrived at Eads Hall, the Education building.

In a few short months, I would graduate with my B.A. in Education. I was eager to be launched across the high seas to teach abroad. With graduation day looming four months ahead, I had signed a contract to teach one year in Peoria, Illinois to fulfill the requirement on my letter of intent to teach the following year in Caracas, Venezuela.

As we were bidding each other farewell, this charming young man, whom I now knew was Howard Lincks, stopped me long enough to inquire about calling me.

That very evening he called and invited me to the newly released movie *On the Waterfront*, starring Marlon Brando. Of course, I accepted, as I enjoyed dating interesting young men and learning about their lives. After all, what girl wouldn't enjoy being taken out to dinner, movies, and cultural events? I sure did, as long as my dates stayed at arm's length.

Wedding bells were ringing for many of my friends. I delighted in the privilege of being a bridesmaid in five weddings. But walking down the aisle to the tune of *Here Comes the Bride* was not in *my* plan. I had lived with four different families in my twenty-one years of growing up. I had observed those relationships. NO – marriage did *not* appear to me to be the wedded bliss my girlfriends imagined it to be.

On graduation day in May of 1955, I walked to the

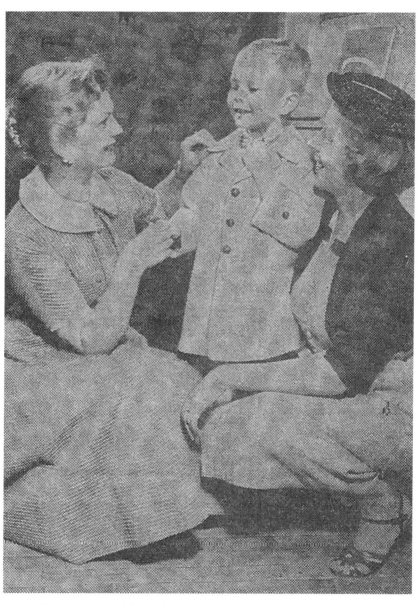

My first year teaching kindergarten at Loucks School in Peoria, Illinois. This photo was published in the local paper.

podium to accept my longed-for diploma from Chancellor Ethan Shipley. Grasping my treasured sheepskin in hand and harboring a heart full of triumph, I was on my way to fulfilling my goals. Visions of shining seas taking me to far away places sparkled like diamonds in my mind.

The sweet fragrance of lilac bushes and blooming trees filled the spring air. Cotton-ball clouds dotted the azure blue sky. These matched the euphoria surrounding my proud mother and me perfectly. I had fulfilled her dreams and aspirations of obtaining a college degree. Remember, Mother's mantra was "Get an education, and you will never have to worry about being able to support yourself." Right then and there, we both gloried in that accomplishment.

I was off to Peoria for my first job teaching kindergarten at Loucks school. In the midst of packing up a four-year accumulation of stuff, a familiar voice called out.

"Can I help?" Instantly, I knew it was Howie, the affectionate name I now called him. He wanted to make sure we could remain in touch. My jam-packed car stood waiting.

Bidding me farewell, a heartfelt admission emitted from his lips and his heart. "I love you." Drawing a deep breath and controlling my heart, I admitted to myself I was falling in love with him. But also in my mind was an awareness I had career commitments – and dreams – to fulfill.

Admittedly, this charismatic architectural student displayed many admirable qualities. Howie's commitment to family shone through his dedication to taking his precious three-year-old niece, Debby Frank, to Sunday school every week. He was also committed to church, to a strong work ethic, to the arts, and to sports, the latter two in which he excelled. Finally, Howie exhibited a contagious sense of humor that especially appealed to me. I felt that had been lacking in my life.

All these desirable attributes I had observed while dating seemed to be neatly wrapped up into this one package labeled Howard Lincks.

Throughout the fall of 1955 Howie would call, write, and come regularly to Peoria to visit. That Christmas, he proposed. Madly in love with him by this time, I accepted his offer on one condition: no marriage until I fulfilled my commitment to teach in Venezuela.

"If you go to Venezuela, we will never get married!" he proclaimed with such vehemence, it startled me. My inner voice screamed, "No, no, no! I can't give up my carefully laid plans!"

I had it all laid out. I wanted to go and teach in Europe. But first I would need to meet the requirement: three years of teaching experience. Finishing up my year in Peoria plus the two-year Venezuela stint would meet that requirement.

After much soul searching, love won out. I shredded the ticket marked "Venezuela" and opened the book labeled "Howard Lincks."

Reverend Allan Van Cleve, my pastor, united us in marriage on a warm sunny day in August 1956. The lofty, gray-steepled First Presbyterian Church of Lewistown bulged to capacity with family and friends from near and

Howard and I at our engagement party.

Our wedding in the First Presbyterian Church of Lewistown in August 1956.

far. I floated down the aisle in my pearl-beaded gown and flowing train to meet my handsome groom, Howie.

Our guests lavished congratulations and best wishes upon us. Then we were off to our week-long honeymoon at a preserve in northern Illinois – two blissfully happy, clueless, strong-willed young people set to start a life together.

We were soon to learn what author and lecturer Florence Littauer so aptly stated: "After every wedding comes a marriage." Returning from our honeymoon, we moved in with Howie's parents until our house was completed.

After the greetings, his mother turned abruptly to me. "Give Howard's white dress shirts to me. They are very expensive. I will take care of them."

I immediately looked at Howie, fully expecting him to say, "Mother, Susie is my wife now, and she will take care of my clothes."

Instead, he looked like he hadn't even heard what she said. I stood there in utter shock. Disappointment and indignation gripped me. Taking a deep breath, I began mentally preparing to stand up for myself.

Then suddenly a flash of remembrance interrupted my resolve. Each week during my high school years, Mother had required me to iron my stepfather's five white shirts. And I remembered — *I hated ironing starched white shirts.* With a big smile on my face, I quickly handed Mother Lincks her son's precious shirts and offered a "Thank you!" For the next twelve years, I gleefully sent Howie's shirts to Mother Lincks.

The spring prior to our wedding, Mother Lincks had managed to foist her will upon us, getting us to begin building our own home. Father Lincks had dreamed of moving out of the big city of St. Louis. They had purchased a small three-acre plot of land, complete with barn, in St. Louis County. He wanted to build a home there and raise Shetland ponies.

Mother Lincks kept dragging her feet, reluctantly playing along with his dream. Now she saw a golden opportunity to get out of the situation. "Hein (German for Henry)," she announced one day, "Let's give the land to Howard and loan him money to build a home there."

Father Lincks slowly allowed his dream to fade away. Desperate to fill his aching heart, he suddenly became excited with her idea. "Indeed, what a magnanimous thing to do for our son and his bride-to-be," he reasoned.

Howie immediately began designing our home. With plans in hand, he arrived in Peoria one day and proudly presented his blueprints to me. I wondered, *"How on earth can I possibly visualize a house from these drawings?"* They were Greek to me!

I proceeded to bombard Howie with a ton of questions. He patiently tried to help me visualize what those white lines on the bright blue paper represented. I confess – planning a big wedding and attending bridal showers was my focus. Admittedly, I thought it all a very thoughtful and generous gift from his parents.

But the Lincks family obsessed over this project. My phone rang off its hook. "Susie, you must come to St. Louis immediately!" came the calls, again and again.

Decisions for our home bombarded me day in and day out.

"You need to choose what baseboarding you want."

"This weekend you must pick out the kitchen cabinets."

"Decide what color you want to paint the walls."

"Next weekend we must decide what heating system we want."

"What tile and color do you want for the bathrooms?"

Help! What a challenge! I was caught in the midst of my first year of teaching school, planning a wedding, and now trying to making house decisions! At a mere 23 years old, I was simply clueless. Mother Lincks sensed my total lack of knowledge concerning house construction. She was in her glory! She had thwarted Hein's moving ideas. Now she could exert a major influence in decorating our home.

During our first year of marriage, I quickly realized Mother Lincks reigned supreme in the Lincks family. Soon after we arrived home from our honeymoon, Howie's family gathered for a meal. When we finished, we remained around the kitchen table – Howie's only sister, Audrey, her husband Lou, Mother and Father Lincks, and the two of us.

No surprise – Mother Lincks held court. She embarked upon a lengthy discussion of Howie's former girlfriends. She went into a detailed opinion of each one. I sat there with my heart crying out, *Howie, please, please stop her!* At the end of that grueling dissertation, I spoke up.

"You left one girl friend out."

Mother Lincks whipped her head around, a shocked look on her face. In an indignant voice she demanded, "Who was that?"

In a very matter-of-fact voice, I replied, "Susie Gray Lincks."

She was speechless.

Lou, a serious engineer type, nearly fell off his chair, bursting into laughter. The rest of the family sat in mute silence. They knew I had sealed my doom with Mother Lincks. No doubt they were thinking, *Oh, you foolish girl.*

For three months we lived with Howard's parents, sleeping on a mattress on the floor of Mother Lincks' office. Most of the time we were away from the house, as we were engulfed in the building and design of our own home. We squeezed every free minute out of our hectic schedules. Five days a week, Howie was off to his architectural classes at Washington University. I was teaching kindergarten at Reavis school in Affton. Work on the home consumed our evenings and weekends so we could complete enough of the interior to move in. There was precious little time devoted to getting to know each other better and to building our relationship.

I learned something about Howie at my first Reavis school teachers meeting, and it shocked me. A third-grade teacher approached me and asked, "Who is your husband?" When I told her, she stared at me with a mixture of awe and disbelief.

"You married 'The Toe,' our Cleveland High School hero?"

My blank expression proved obvious to her. She went on to explain that Howard received that nickname because he had saved so many football games. His years of playing soccer made him a savvy field goal kicker, often scoring the winning point for many games.

Introduced to the game of soccer by his father at a young age, Howie rapidly excelled in the sport – so much so, that he aspired to become an Olympic team player. While, unfortunately, this dream was obliterated by a serious football knee injury in high school, he still remained active in metropolitan sport leagues for many years.

Fall filled our world with exciting colors matching our spirit of celebration. We did it!! We had finished up our home's interior enough for us to live there. It was one step up from camping out. Our electricity came from a temporary electric pole in what would later become our front yard.

Picking up our mail on my way home from school one day, I noticed we had just received an electric bill. Walking through the door, I casually handed it to Howie. His vehement response shocked me.

"Don't give me that bill! You pay the bills."

Neither one of us had ever seen a household bill. His mother was the household *and* business bookkeeper in his family. My stepfather Martin had sent our bills automatically to his law office. We shoved that bill at each other until the electric company threatened to shut our service down for non- payment. "Little" incidences like this uncovered our vastly different backgrounds. And they later led to profound consequences in our marriage.

Our home in St. Louis under a blanket of snow.

One Friday after a full week of teaching my ninety-plus energetic kindergarteners, I arrived home to find our front porch loaded with plants. It didn't take much to figure out the plants came from Mother and Father Lincks. While we appreciated their generosity, we also needed to rest over the weekend, since both of us went at full speed during the week.

I didn't want to be ungrateful, but this happened again and again.

One particular evening Howie arrived home late. He found me down on my knees planting. I looked up at him and declared, "I hate working in the dirt!"

Howie's brash retort smacked me in the gut and jolted me into reality. "Well, you have three acres to hate."

Howie's harsh words ended up serving as a catalyst for my deliberate action, and a chain reaction. I enrolled in an adult night class to learn about flower arranging. This led to joining a garden club.

As a newlywed, I didn't have extra money to purchase flowers for the club's flower arranging workshops. Instead, I started planting flowers. In 1962, my best friend, Jeanne Flynn, and I started a garden club. We named it Gateway Garden club after the St. Louis Gateway arch, which was in construction at the time. We also started a junior garden club. All this contributed to my life-long love of gardening.

At eighty-six years of age, I still bask in the enjoyment of digging in my garden.

We had spent a year pouring our energy into our new two-bedroom brick house. Finally, the anticipated day arrived.

"It's finished," we shouted, collapsing in fatigue and satisfaction. We sighed with weariness and glowed at our accomplishment. Now we could relax and enjoy the fruits of our labor.

Howie arrived home, carrying a large box and grinning from ear to ear.

"Happy Anniversary, Susie. On our first anniversary I chose a gift for you which will give us pleasure together for a lifetime."

I opened the gift full of anticipation. To my shock and consternation, I unwrapped a complete set of ladies golf clubs with golf lessons attached. My jaw just hung there for a moment. It was a rare moment when I simply didn't know what to say.

Then I uttered, "They are beautiful, Howie. But neither of us play golf...."

Howie responded without missing a beat. "In five years, I hope to have the business managed so that I can come home early and we can hit the links. In the meantime, you can enjoy learning to play by joining a lady's golf league."

It flashed through my mind at that moment what he, a born athlete, was likely thinking, *Susie will hopefully have her game up to speed so I can enjoy playing my first game of golf with her by then.* True, we did play many games of golf together during our marriage.

It was a short time into our first year of marriage when a particular incident shocked and hurt me deeply. Maye Oshiro and her husband George stopped by one evening to see our new home. Maye and I taught kindergarten at Reavis School together. Howie, as usual, was out playing ball. We chatted quite awhile, thinking Howie would return while Maye and George were still at our house. As it was getting late they needed to leave.

As I stepped out the door to bid them farewell, I accidently locked myself out. They wanted to stay with me until Howie returned. I thanked them for their concern and assured them Howie would be home soon.

But that wasn't the case. I sat outside on our cold concrete steps until 3 am! He finally arrived safely, but completely drunk. He didn't even notice me as he stumbled through the door and crashed into bed. Little did I realize then that this would become a pattern throughout our life together. Sadly, I also came to discover that no matter how upset I was and how much I tried to discuss this behavior, my worries only fell upon deaf ears.

After a year and a half at our new home on 12227 Adams Drive, we got a real shock: we were soon to be a family of three. In fact, I was a full four months pregnant!

I had been experiencing some physical symptoms, lethargy and missed periods. The thought of possibly being pregnant had flashed through my mind. I had discussed it with my mother. My physical body showed no sign of change so I had quickly dismissed the possibility.

In fact, during this time, I had urged Howie to quit his job and focus exclusively on finishing his architecture degree. I was willing to take on the full financial responsibility for our family. Little did we know a new life was growing inside of me. Howie paid the Washington University tuition for that fall. We were excitedly anticipating the completion of his thesis and his graduation from architecture school in the spring.

Fall arrived with Howie off to class and my kindergarteners arriving for school. At the same time I was experiencing some excruciating leg cramps. I quickly made a doctor's appointment. As the doctor listened to my complaints and examined me, he said, "You are at least four months pregnant."

In shock, I said, "Doctor, I can't be."

"Well," he said, "You are not growing watermelons."

Back at school, I told my best friend Jeanne Flynn,

Jill and I.

the third grade teacher, "I must talk to you ASAP." Telling her I was pregnant, I said, "What am I going to do? If I tell Howie, he will say he must forfeit his tuition and go back to work."

In the midst of my panic, Jeanne brought me back to reality. "How long do you think you can go without telling him?" That's when I realized I must tell him that very evening.

At dinner we shared our day's events. Then I drew in a deep breath and said, "Howie, I am four months pregnant."

After a stunned silence, he said, "I must quit school."

"No!" I cried. "There must be something else we can do." God actually ended up using this situation much differently than we anticipated. We did find a way through this tenuous yet exciting period.

Our baby girl, lovely big brown eyes looking up at us expectantly, arrived on January 21, 1958.

Mary Jill Lincks entered this world through the same hospital where her father had arrived 27 years earlier. Howie scooped her up with such tenderness and love, bringing the two of us home while beaming with pride and joy. Something beautiful emerged in Howie that day. I glimpsed the tender, sweet, sensitive, artistic side of my husband I had seen before.

Jill proved a happy, contented baby and became the shining light of our life together. Howie seemed to relish his new role as father. After school in the morning and work in the afternoon, Howie would arrive home, gathering Jill in his big bear arms, holding her tightly.

At the same time, our boxer dog, Roy, seemed to be sulking. He'd hold up his paw, limping around with a sad look on his face. We thought his paw was hurt until the day we saw him switch paws. Then we realized he was simply faking it. Roy clearly missed our undivided attention. In time, however, Roy grew to love Jill. As she began crawling, he allowed her to climb all over him and lay on top of him.

At six months old, we decided to christen Jill. The family all gathered to witness the occasion at our Presbyterian church in Kirkwood, Missouri. Jill seemed to bask in all the unsolicited attention. We celebrated together her dedication to Jesus Christ throughout the day.

Four short days later, tragedy struck. Father Lincks collapsed and died of a brain aneurysm. His sudden death provoked a great upheaval. The Henry Lincks contracting business was a small family business. Howie had worked part time for his father throughout high school and college. This made him able to step in and manage the business.

Having just completed his architectural thesis, Howie emerged receiving several awards for his outstanding architectural designs. He was looking forward to becoming a full-fledged architect after completion as an understudy.

We were all mourning Father Lincks' death. In the midst of all this, a career crisis for Howie was looming.

Would Howie pursue his architectural career dream, or instead run the family business?

The business desperately needed a foreman to survive. Mother Lincks put tremendous pressure on Howie to take over the reins of the business. His countenance reflected his torment. With heavy hearts, we saw his architectural talent and creativity slowly buried in bricks and mortar. We were not only mourning his father's death, we were mourning the death of his career dream.

Contention and strife marked the next 16 years of Howie's life as he tried to lead the company under his mother's iron-clad will. Her position as business manager in the company led to her having full control of our finances as well.

Unfulfilled dreams mixed with his mother's toxic interference in both his professional and personal life proved a bitter poison, leading to Howie's growing resort to the bottle. Even though Howie had always been a "boy's boy," full of energy, passion and enthusiasm, a sharp edge developed during this time, as he saw the life he had always envisioned slipping away.

Now don't get me wrong. Howie was a person of great enthusiasm and humor. He was never a pessimist, grumbling within about this situation. In fact, most people had no idea of the internal war raging inside him. Alcohol mollified this fire. Often, it actually added to his jovial nature. But, still, it eventually found a way to wind its sinister grip around Howie's life, and around us all.

One year had passed after saying goodbye to Father Lincks and Howie's anticipated architectural career. We were adjusting to a changed life and working on our marriage. Suddenly, a sweet fragrance enveloped us with good news. We were pregnant again!

With that wonderful news, I made the difficult decision to retire from teaching. It was a hard choice. I loved teaching those vivacious kindergarteners! I always aimed to give one hundred percent of myself to them, giving them the best possible introduction to the love of learning and school. My dilemma was how to give my all to both my kindergarteners and my family. Instantly, I knew the answer. My family came first, and yet there was a deep ache in my heart saying goodbye to teaching.

Eight months later, a mere day past my 27th birthday, we welcomed Merri Holly Lincks into our lives on December 18th, 1959.

As young parents, Dr. Spock's book, *Baby and Child Care*, was considered the gold standard for learning how to care properly for children. It also was the only reference book available at the time. We followed his specific instructions for introducing the second child into our family. Dr. Spock told us the father is to carry the baby into the home, freeing up the mother to give her undivided attention to the older child.

Me and my girls, shortly after Holly's arrival in our family!

Holly (left) and Jill (right) grew up best of friends, as you might be able to tell from this photo!

Howie happily carried Holly in our home as I threw my arms around Jill. Instantly she squealed and tore herself out of my embrace. Running after her father, she yelled at the top of her voice, "The baby, the baby!"

It seems sibling jealousy or resentment never entered our home. That is, except with our dog, Roy. Just as he had done with Jill's arrival, Roy did whatever he could to get our attention, including putting on a show of pain in his paws. But regardless, Jill adored her blue-eyed, towheaded younger sister.

As Holly grew, Jill's voice resonated throughout our home. "Mommy, Mommy, don't scold her." Yes, I was a strict Mommy. Taking the girls shopping before Easter, Jill begged, "Mommy, Mommy, can I buy Holly a fuzzy white Easter bunny?"

As little children, Jill and Holly happily played and sang together. I taught them many kindergarten songs. Once, when we were attending the Orange Bowl in Fort Lauderdale, Florida, the girls were skipping along, hand-in-hand. Several people stopped us to comment on their talent. One even told us, "You should take them to Hollywood!"

We were fascinated as we witnessed their individual talents and personalities blossom.

Holly yearned to do everything her sister did. She squirmed as I held her on my lap at Jill's ballet class. In frustration, I allowed her to stand by my chair to mimic her sister's pirouettes and pliés. Excitement filled our home when at three years of age she was allowed to enter the class. Several years later, the piano teacher arrived to teach

Jill. Holly listened closely. When Jill's lesson ended, Holly would sit right down and play the exact same song.

The girls were the joy of my life. Of course, we faced the normal growing-up challenges with them. But being a stay-at-Mom, I could give them my total devotion.

Howie's athletic prowess automatically influenced our lives. The first night of predicted freezing temperatures propelled him into action. He spent the entire night framing and filling in our lower patio with water. By morning, he had created our very own ice skating rink! Howie taught our girls, at two and four years old, to be proficient ice skaters. We all enjoyed skating together on our rink as well as at public ice skating rinks and neighboring ponds during those frigid winter months.

At home, Howie had programmed our television for all sports. The girls and I grew to become great fans of the Olympics. Football dominated our Sunday afternoons. Howie often had to call me in out of the garden to see the game. Our various dogs, cats and rabbits would frequently join us. At intermission, we'd break for a snack. Penny, our horse, watching us from her feeding box in the field close to our home, would kick it hard to get our attention. "I want some of my oats and hay to snack with you," we imagined her saying.

Jill excelled at sports, much like her Dad. When she was three, she became an avid swimmer and diver. In high school, she was on the diving team. She played little league softball. She was the only girl who played ball with the neighborhood boys. Because she was so active, she

Jill (left) and Holly (right) enjoying their home-made ice skating rink.

frequently broke or sprained things. We were emergency room regulars.

The part of school Jill enjoyed was purely social. She wasn't much into school, per se. Part of this, we came to realize, was a result of a mild case of dyslexia. Creative and angsty, Jill pushed many boundaries, not unlike her father.

Holly, in contrast, took more after me. She was more subdued and even-keeled. Holly sought to always be on top of her class academically. She had her sights set on a career in physical therapy from her early high school years, and she calculated what she needed to do to achieve that goal.

In her second grade year, Jill came bursting through our front door one day. She was ablaze with excitement. "Daddy, Mommy, I want to be a Camp Fire Girl!"

I took a deep breath, giving my mind time to slowly let go of my vision of my girls being Girl Scouts as I had been. Both Howie and I felt strongly that we needed to give Jill and Holly freedom to make their own choices and not be shackled by family expectations.

"Tell us about Camp Fire Girls, Jill," we responded.

Her enthusiasm bubbled over as she spoke. To see our cherished daughter, a struggling student, filled with such joy and enthusiasm, was a breath of fresh air for us. We didn't realize it then, but when we agreed to let Jill become a Camp Fire Girl, we embarked upon a ten-year, adventure-filled journey with the program.

Not surprisingly, Holly, too, became a Camp Fire Girl when she entered second grade. I became a Camp Fire Girl leader for her group. Howie served on the board of the Greater St. Louis Area Camp Fire Girl Council. The Council met weekly in our home. Every year, our garage filled almost to the ceiling with Russell Stover Chocolates as we entered into the fundraising season.

We made monthly excursions to care for our group's adopted invalid lady in the South County Rest Home. The girls entertained their parents at the annual Camp Fire Girls dinner. They planned the menu, cooked, and served the food. Then they held us captive as they performed a show written and directed by them.

With Camp Fire Girls we spent two weeks on a dude ranch in Gunnison, Colorado and attended the Camp Fire National Convention in San Antonio, Texas. We delivered meals to shut-ins for Meals-On-Wheels and helped with many more individual activities to earn beads for their Camp Fire Girl uniforms, all to fulfill the Camp Fire motto, "Give Service." Our Camp Fire Girls rode on their first plane, flying to Canada, to learn about another land and culture.

One of my Camp Fire girls wrote a note to me not long ago, reflecting upon her experience:

"I have such fond memories of our Camp Fire days. In fact, when my own daughter became a Girl Scout, I was reminded of the many activities we participated in as Camp Fire Girls. I think

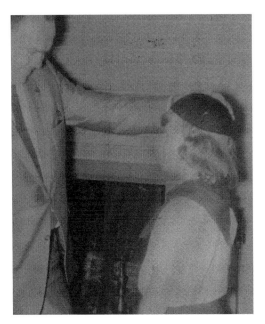

Jill in her Camp Fire gear with her father.

Holly selling candy to fundraise with the Camp Fire Girls.

through Camp Fire Girls I learned what it is to be charitable. You have no idea how many lives you touched. I now have two children who help with Meals-On-Wheels, AMC cancer research, recycling, etc. Also, one of my children's favorite activities is staying home and making s'mores over the fire, much like we used to do in our Camp Fire Girls group."

I remember well how much Howie enjoyed the season of Halloween. Jill and Holly were blessed with a very imaginative and artistic father who delighted in making up their faces in great detail as well as seating them before the fireplace, turning out the lights and telling them scary stories. I particularly remember when Howie made-up Holly to look just like a China doll to accompany her Chinese costume.

One year Howie and I planned a special Halloween party for the Camp Fire Girls. Dressed as a ghost, I kidnapped each girl from their home, blindfolded them, and drove them to our home. Howie greeted them with a deep, menacing voice while shaking their hands with a rubber glove filled with ice. The girls trembled, but, after we removed their blindfolds, their relief was palpable. They enjoyed bobbing for apples, dipping themselves downward to grab the shiny red apples in their mouths, hands behind their backs. They played guessing games, trying to figure out the contents of Halloween-themed items in a sack. Black and orange reigned supreme on the dessert table.

As a family, we maintained an active community life. It's almost as if our car seemed to know its own way to the world-famous St. Louis Art Museum, the City Zoo, the Missouri Historical Society, and Webster Grove's Theater, where both children took a range of classes.

Howie and I were officers in the Concord Grade School PTA in addition to our service with Campfire Girls and Gateway Garden Club. I also sat on the board of the Open Space Council, developing parks for metropolitan St. Louis. Howie relished his involvement with the Concord Lions Club.

As members of First Presbyterian Church of Kirkwood, Missouri, not far from our home in Concord Village, all four of us kept active. The girls attended Sunday school, Vacation Bible School, and sang in the children's choir. I directed Vacation Bible School for several years, and frequently taught Sunday school. I even became an ordained deacon.

For a couple years, Howie served as leader for the Couples Group at First Pres Kirkwood. One time, a young guest speaker came and related to us his fascinating journey of reaching out to international exchange students in the U.S. What he shared intrigued us, birthing a common passion to serve in the program ourselves.

One morning, while Jill and Holly were in fifth and

Jill (left) and Holly (right) singing in the church children's choir at First Presbyterian Church of Kirkwood.

seventh grades, we sat at our breakfast table reading the local *South County Journal*. Our eyes fell on an article entitled *Families Sought to Host AFS Students From Abroad.* This article immediately propelled us into action. With one quick phone call we learned AFS stood for American Field Service. Their purpose was to give students around the world cross-cultural experiences.

Through that phone call, we were able to set up an appointment with the board of review. The reviewers came to our home so they could assess whether or not we were suited as hosts for their program.

Shortly thereafter, a packet arrived, informing us we were accepted into the program to host an international student for one year. Our student, Kevin Tatz, was set to arrive in August from Johannesburg, South Africa!

Great anticipation, excitement and wonder filled each of us that hot, humid late August day when it was time to head to St. Louis International airport to pick Kevin up. At 12 and 10 years old, respectively, Jill and Holly wondered aloud what life would be like with a teenage boy in our home. Howard looked forward to having another man in the house. And I pondered having a son.

As we walked down the gateway our eyes fell upon a young man, slight of build, with curly black hair. He stood amidst a pile of luggage, looking a bit apprehensive. We all exclaimed at once, "That must be Kevin!" We immediately clustered around him with warm greetings, attempting to put him at ease and wash away his fear and trepidation.

Upon reflection much later, I realize we all had

expected Kevin to be white from the moment we learned about him, even though in the early 1970's South Africa's white population amounted to less than 20 percent of its total (and is even lower now). I think this is because (1) we learned from AFS Kevin was coming from a private boy's school, so we imagined him coming from a more privileged household; and (2) Jill and Holly's schools were notably all white. We had not planned for that; it's simply how things had worked out for us.

What we didn't anticipate, however, is what we learned on the ride home from the airport that day. Kevin was an orthodox Jew! From birth he had lived in a tight-knit Jewish neighborhood while attending a private Jewish grade school and high school. In fact, we were his first encounter with a Gentile family.

Kevin told us his father, a dermatologist, had fled from England during WWII and settled in Johannesburg. Howie met my wide eyes, momentarily exchanging identical thoughts. We were bringing a young, zealous Orthodox Jewish teenager into our predominantly German South County home in metropolitan St. Louis to live with our family of German heritage!

The year was 1971, twenty-six years following the end of WWII. There were certainly strong lingering emotions and prejudices from that tragic event. I thought to myself, this should prove to be a fascinating and challenging journey for us all.

For Kevin there were a myriad of adjustments. He was raised with many servants, and now he would be

Kevin (center), our AFS student, with our family.

cleaning his own room and helping us maintain an acre of lawn and garden. "No swimming pool or pool man or yard man? No cook or housekeeper?" he inquired.

Smiling, we responded, "Ah, no." Welcome to our humble home in mid-America, Kevin.

"Where is the synagogue?" he asked almost immediately. "Because I walk to synagogue at the beginning of the Jewish Sabbath every Friday night as required by Orthodox law."

"Sad to tell you, Kevin," we responded, "the Orthodox synagogue is a forty-five minute drive from our home."

He proceeded to tell us he could not eat any meat and milk products together or eat any meat cooked in a pan milk had ever been cooked in. And, of course, no pork. Drawing a deep breath as we digested this information, we asked, "So, Kevin, have you brought your separate pots, pans, and dishes with you?"

He looked at us incredulously.

So began our year of adventure into the world of an orthodox Jewish teenager.

Kevin practiced all the Biblical Old Testament festivals and events. It was October when the first ceremonial event called the Festival of Booths occurred. This is an Old Testament celebration of the harvest. Kevin felt compelled to attend an Orthodox Jewish synagogue for this event. Because of a work conflict, Howard was unable to attend. I was the one to take Kevin to the only Orthodox synagogue in all of the large metropolitan St. Louis area.

As I drove with Kevin through the Friday night rush-hour trek to University City, the predominantly Jewish settlement, I contemplated spending a delightful time by myself at the nearby upscale shopping mecca while Kevin would be in the synagogue. But Kevin made plain his desire for me to attend synagogue with him that night.

"Oh, please, Mum," he pleaded, using the endearing South African title he had bestowed upon me. He assured me that even though men and women were not allowed to worship together, I could just follow the other women. He had completely forgotten they would instead be home cooking and making preparations for the Sabbath. Hearing his pleading voice ringing in my ears, I saw my dream of leisurely window shopping drifting away.

As we approached the synagogue, I noticed Kevin slouch down in the car. Alarmed, I asked him, "Kevin are you ill?"

He replied, "No, but no one should see me riding in a car." He explained he was breaking Jewish law by riding in a car at the beginning of the Sabbath. From sundown Friday night to sundown Saturday night, their sacred Sabbath, they were to be totally focused on God. The Old Testament law required that absolutely nothing disturb this devotion Not even turning on or off a light!

The evening was one of the most awkward moments of my life. There I sat, all alone in the women's section, fervently praying my blonde hair would miraculously turn coal black. The little old Jewish men would whip their skull capped heads in my direction, glaring at me over the waist-high divider between us. They rocked back and forth, fingering their prayer shawl tassels and reciting their prayers.

Kevin, too, found the evening excruciating. The congregation reacted in shock when he told them he was living with us, a Gentile family. They told him, "Kevin, you are committing a grievous sin against God. You must leave that family immediately!"

But where was he to go? None of them offered to take him into one of *their* homes.

It was through that evening of crisis and pain our relationship grew deeper. The shared experience seemed to seal our commitment to each other.

It turns out, our year together was filled to overflowing with God's love, compassion, and mercy. Every Friday night, Howard faithfully took Kevin to an Orthodox synagogue less strict in its religious requirements. He ate food cooked and served off our utensils and dishes. One concession I made was not to cook milk and meat products together. We were even written up in *The Jewish Light*, a St. Louis Jewish periodical, for keeping a kosher kitchen. Before meals, we began to say grace in both the Jewish and Christian traditions. At Hanukkah and Christmas we enjoyed a Menorah service and our candlelight Advent devotions.

When Kevin's day of departure came a year later, we found ourselves all hugging, kissing, clinging, and crying as we said our goodbyes. That scene of letting go of our Orthodox Jewish adopted son and brother from Johannesburg, South Africa forever etched itself on all of our hearts and minds. It helped all of us better grasp the largeness of God's overpowering love.

During Kevin's year with us, we discussed God and the Bible a great deal. He, as a devout Orthodox Jew with a Rabbi grandfather, had an outstanding grasp of the Old Testament Scriptures. These discussions made me vividly aware of my own lack of knowledge of the New Testament and even my understanding of the Christian faith. Kevin had become the catalyst in my quest to better understand God. At the same time, I began to question some of the decisions I had made in my own life, realizing I had made some poor ones along the way.

Living with a functional alcoholic led me to a time of personal crisis as well. I felt as if I just couldn't continue this life of Howie's nightly bar stops while our family dinner was waiting. I was weary of always waiting up until Howie staggered through the door. I sought God, even though I didn't have a personal relationship with him yet. I cried out to him. He saw my heart of love for my girls and my desire to do no damage to their lives. I saw my answer clearly: sacrifice your desire for happiness, and stay in this marriage. That settled the matter in my heart forever.

As I sat teaching Bible stories to six-year-olds in the elegant and cavernous First Presbyterian Church of Kirkwood Missouri, my heart cried out. *What are all these*

Bible stories really all about? What is all this church work really all about? There has to be more.

Sharing my deep question with my friend and neighbor, Esther, she confessed she had similar questions.

It was two years later that Esther called and excitedly exclaimed, "I've found it. I've found what we were missing. Jesus is alive."

"No way, Esther," I answered. "He died over 2,000 years ago."

"Yes, Sue, but after his resurrection he sent his Holy Spirit to live in our hearts when we truly accept him as our Lord and Savior. Read Luke, Chapter Three and John, Chapter Three in your Bible."

As a person who did believe the Bible was the infallible word of God, I searched those chapters of Scripture, studied five different versions them, prayed, attended Esther's Bible study, and listened to testimonies of changed lives and healings.

I became convinced of God's power: namely, that Father God, his son, Jesus, and the Holy Spirit are all wrapped up in one package – the Trinity, three-in-one. After Jesus' resurrection from the dead, he sent the Holy Spirit to earth to live in our hearts. I finally confessed, "Lord, I know I need a personal Savior. I've certainly failed at running my own life."

"Jesus, I confess I am a sinner in need of you to save me. Please pour your Holy Spirit into my heart and guide my life." Being "born again," as described by Jesus in the book of John, Chapter Three, meant I was a new creature in

Christ. I became filled with an insatiable desire to study the Bible, his Word given to us. From then on, the Holy Spirit, my teacher, illuminated God's word for me. Those words from the Bible began to burst into life with such gripping clarity.

Once I let go of the control of my life, amazing things began to happen. My whole outlook and attitude toward Howard and some of his actions changed. Our marriage became more harmonious. Our next five years together transformed from serious struggling and battling to a unity and peace I hadn't thought possible.

At the same time, Howard experienced a wake-up call in his own life. Howie continued to drink until the late night or early morning with the guys after the Concord Lions Club meetings. But one particular night as I waited for him to come home, I was at work in the kitchen. Suddenly, the door was flung open and several of his buddies helped Howie into the kitchen. He staggered, crashing into one of the kitchen cabinets, extremely inebriated, and then fell to the floor, writhing in pain.

That severe knock on his head brought him to the realization that he had to change. He promptly started resigning from activities that easily enticed him to drink. Lion's Club was one of them.

Letting go of my controlling ways and growing in my personal relationship with my Jesus caused me to dive deeper and deeper into God's ultimate love for me in an intimate, personal way. It enabled me to love Howard unconditionally. The reality of Christ's obedience and sacrifice on the cross because of his personal love for all mankind filled me with such freedom, ecstasy, and joy. Our marriage transformed into a deeper love over the next few years.

Some time later, I joined a small women's Bible Study. But the Holy Spirit kept saying, "Study the Book of Job." I had no desire to study the Old Testament book, especially now with Jesus alive in my heart. God's persistent voice – "Study Job" – challenged and shocked me into examining my heart.

Was my confession of faith real? Yes, absolutely. I was certain God, Jesus and the Holy Spirit, the triune 3-in-1 God, resided in my heart. Immediately I jumped into studying the Book of Job.

Imagine my shock as I opened to Job's tragedies! My new life was now filled with spontaneous, joyful expectations. I kept pondering the question, *Why, indeed, would my Holy Spirit insist I study Job?*

One reason might have been because God wanted me to grasp the depth of God's love for Job so I would better understand the depth of His love for me. He also wanted me to comprehend his mercy and grace better. In his mercy and compassion, I believe He wanted me to be spiritually fortified for the what would happen just ahead.

For sheer amazement coupled with heart-wretching tragedy propelled our family into the next four years.

One day, Howie rushed through the front door, bursting with excitement. "Susie, Jill, Holly! I've got a huge surprise for you! I'm taking you to Germany!"

It was the spring of 1974. Howie's soccer team, along with their families, were headed to the famous World Cup in Frankfurt.

We spent two weeks in Germany. Our teenage girls had a blast with the other teens on the tour. The first week was with the soccer team and their families, totally wrapped up in the world of soccer, or "football," as it is known outside of the U.S. Indeed, the intense football soccer culture in Germany swept us away. Such passion and dedication!

The second week we rented a VW bug. We four enjoyed the picturesque southern part of the country. While in the Bavarian area of Germany, we spent a night with Martin and his family, one of the high school exchange students we had hosted. The girls hung out with Martin and his friends while I enjoyed the evening with Martin's grandmother, mother, and father. Howie, instead, was out with his soccer buddies.

Thursday morning following our return home, Howie was out on the golf course again. I found myself immersed in the study of Job. Our phone began ringing insistently, but I ignored it to keep focused. Finally, I gave in and picked up the receiver. A wave of shock coursed through me.

"Sue, this is Joe. Come to Barnes Hospital immediately. Howard collapsed on the golf course and has been rushed by ambulance to Emergency."

Joe's words echo in my mind even now, decades later.

Following emergency surgery, two days later Dr. Hullett walked gravely into the hospital room. The news he brought overwhelmed us all. "Howard has colon cancer. He has about four months to live."

We sat there in stunned silence, in total shock. As we drew deep breaths, trying to process this death sentence, Howard immediately sprang into his athletic approach, his eye always on winning the game.

"Doctor Hullett, I'm not *dying* with cancer, I'm *living* with cancer. Now tell me what steps you recommend I should take. And, by the way, it's two weeks until Christmas. I want out of this hospital, as I plan to take my family to Florida for the holidays. Susie, get on the phone and make reservations at a motel on Sanibel Island, Florida."

Howard, "The Toe," the star football scorer, was back on the playing Field of Life.

Yet I sat there saying to myself, *Lord, how can this be? Not again!*

For during my study of Job two years earlier, my phone had been ringing nonstop. It was Martin, my stepfather. "Susie, come to Graham Hospital in Canton [Illinois] immediately. Your mother is going to have emergency surgery." Her diagnosis was cancer with nine months to live.

Overlapping this time, my stepfather was actually dying of diabetes and heart disease. Now, Mother was in

Heaven in the presence of Jesus. She entered Jesus' arms January 26, 1972. Martin had received a miraculous aortic valve replacement, though we had no idea how it would hold. And now this!

The purpose God had for me to dive deep into the Book of Job suddenly became crystal clear. God's overwhelming, abundant love for me in every detail of my life gripped me deeply. My all-knowing loving Father prepared me personally through the study of Job for the tragedies I now found myself walking through. This realization of the intimacy of our God for each person filled me with the desire to shout it out to the world.

Indeed, His Word, melodious songs of praise, and the flowers all around me continued to sustain and feed me. He consoled me as I spent time in our garden, taking time for rest and rejuvenation while caring for my loved ones.

I remembered the beginning refrain of one of my grandmother's songs, *"I walk in the garden alone while the dew is still on the roses, and He walks with me and He talks with me and He tells me I am His own; And the joy we share as we tarry there, none other has ever known."* The love in those words and now in my personal relationship with Jesus were a source of great strength for me during that tragic season of loss.

No question, God had me firmly in his grip throughout it all. I felt His springs of love flood my soul with mercy and compassion, an incredible gift. He restored me with His strength to once again be a caregiver for my Howie. At the same time, I strove to be sensitive and comforting to my precious teenage girls. They pitched in to help me as well.

What followed were twenty-one months of experimental drugs administered by the oncology department at our distinguished Washington University School of Medicine while Howard *lived* with cancer. He took us to Florida for Christmas; he took us to Arizona for spring vacation; he went on a golf tournament with his golfing buddies; we played golf together; and he continued to work hard running the Henry Lincks Contracting business. He also did architectural design work when the opportunity arose. He pursued his artistic talent through his sketching and watercolor media. He continued his lifelong habit of cracking funny jokes, making everyone laugh and endearing himself to all.

During those months Howard had colostomy surgery and grew progressively thinner. The day arrived when he didn't feel like getting up for work. He demanded I take him to the Barnes Hospital's Emergency Room. After a week in the hospital they released him saying there was nothing further they could do for him.

Once again, the star athlete with his determination and persistence to make the scoring goal proclaimed, "Tomorrow, you will drive me to work." He repeated those words for five days until we realized it would no longer happen.

During the last month of Howard's life, my perceptive teenage daughters frequently told me, "Mom, we'll sit with Dad. You go rest."

This was not the first time I had heard and seen their understanding, helpful hearts. They had understood my same need four years earlier while caring for my mother and then my stepfather. I had journeyed 150 miles each way on weekends to care for my mother while she was dying with cancer. They had grasped the need for those trips, as well as the need for my six-week hospital bedside stints and then home care following my stepfather's open-heart surgery.

Their helpful, loving words still ring in my head, "Mom, we'll do the laundry. Mom, we'll clean the house." The love of my Lord sustained and strengthened me; the loving help of Jill and Holly made it possible for me to care for their father in our home until he saw Jesus face-to-face.

On April 15, 1976, at age 45, Howard fell asleep in my arms, exhausted from playing his game of life, and winning his final goal of eternal life in heaven. Overflowing crowds of family and friends gathered for his funeral. We all believed Howard, with his timely and wonderful sense of humor, must have had a classic joke his first day in heaven: "Thanks Jesus – You saved me from mailing in my taxes today!"

It wasn't long after this, as the girls and I were sitting together with tears in our eyes and hearts, when suddenly a phone call jolted us out of our sadness.

7

Missions Emerging

Agapanthus

Undying love and new birth

Merely five months after Howard died, a surprise phone call brought a welcome and familiar voice from the past. It was Hazel Lee. We had taught together at Reavis School in Affton, Missouri in the late 1950s. She had continued teaching and pursuing her vocation as a watercolor artist while I became a stay-at-home mom.

I had numerous activities during Jill and Holly's school years. They included community service (specifically Open Space Council), gardening, and presenting my crafts and candle making on local television as part of the Greater

Metropolitan St. Louis Garden Club Lecture Series. I also appeared on the local television station's 30-minute Q&A show giving the community information on the development of parks and recreation for the St. Louis Metropolitan Area.

Hazel knew of some of my hobbies. She also knew I was recently widowed. She had a proposal floating around in her head. It might fill a need in my life as well as hers. Excitement and anticipation rising in her voice, she inquired of me, "Sue, have you heard about Lucianna Ross's mission to restore the Village of Kimmswick?"

Hardly pausing to take a breath, she rushed into giving me a brief description of this historical endeavor. Luciana, also known as Mrs. Gladney Ross, was heir to the 7-Up Bottling Company. Her desire for this restoration sprang from happy childhood memories of Kimmswick.

The Village of Kimmswick was founded by Theodore Kimm in 1859. It overlooks the Mississippi River. Kimmswick became a thriving shipping port in the late 1800s. Its picturesque high bluffs above the river became a favorite site. Wealthy sea captains built their elegant homes there. The scene filled people's minds with imaginations of great adventures aboard ships bound for exotic places.

The area also boasted inviting hot springs, turning it into a much sought-after health spa resort. The village of Kimmswick became a favorite weekend retreat for the wealthy families of St. Louis. On bucolic summer weekends, there would be concerts in the park and children's games. Picnics were held on the high bluffs overlooking the Mississippi River.

The excitement Luciana had felt as a child boarding the train in St. Louis with her family bound for Kimmswick had never left her. Lucianna was captivated as she watched the boats floating down the river. She would imagine fantastic adventures aboard ships bound for places she had only heard about. Time had passed it by as new highways arose and criss-crossed the land. Watching her beloved Kimmswick crumble and decay was breaking her heart. She simply could not stand by without taking action. She vowed to start a restoration project.

Upon introduction to Hazel, Lucianna marveled at her artistic talent and, most of all, her passion for preserving history. Hazel was dedicated to establishing a mastodon park near Imperial, Missouri, for many skeletons had been unearthed there. Hazel's efforts had gained attention in the local media of the time. Luciana met with Hazel and challenged her to join her in the restoration of Kimmswick.

The Ziegler General Store, built by local resident Michael Ziegler in 1913, was the first building slated for restoration. The store, once a general merchandise and jewelry repair establishment, now was an empty, dilapidated building badly in need of paint and repair. With Hazel and Luciana's effort, the store took on a new life as The Kimmswick Country Store. After the restoration, it boasted an impressive assortment of antiques and crafts, as well as an accompanying art gallery.

Hazel's timely call and question for me was, "Sue, do you have crafts you can supply me with? Better yet, would like to be a partner in this historic venture?"

Me next to the Kimmswick County Store sign.

The Kimmswick County Store.

My immediate response was an emphatic, "Yes!" to both questions. I knew *I* needed restoration too. My last four years were filled with caring for loved ones dying in my arms.

It was an exhilarating time for us. The Kimmswick Country Store, the first establishment in this restoration, morphed into a hub of activity. Hazel and I were the proprietors. We featured antiques and penny candy in old fashioned glass jars. Hazel hung her paintings in the art gallery. There, we served private luncheons. We cooked, we gardened, we sold, and we served.

Ours was the first of fifty-two restored buildings. In the fall, we featured an apple butter festival. We also held a pumpkin carving contest for the schoolchildren. We held Christmas candlelight tours of the historic homes we decorated in the style of the early 1900s.

Holly, now a high school senior, managed the Sweet Shop. In the tiny one-room log cabin, she sold her own homemade fudge. Each weekend we loaded up our 1967 Camaro and whizzed down Interstate Highway 55 to Kimmswick.

It is now on the National Historic Register. Luciana's childhood memory has been featured on national television. It is host to visitors from around the world. There are house tours, restaurants, bed and breakfasts, a library, and unique gift and craft shops. I am so thankful to have had the privilege of being a tiny cog in the mighty wheels of this historical preservation.

This restoration project was a huge step toward my

own restoration as well.

Every Tuesday morning I loaded my golf clubs into my car and headed for the golf course. Playing in the local Ladies Golf League was especially exhilarating one particular morning. Finishing my eighteen holes, I headed for the club house for a Coke. I ran into Mildred Gubany, an acquaintance, who asked if I had a bit of time to chat.. Her request surprised me, as I barely knew her. As we sat down she spoke up. "I understand you are a widow. I have a gentleman I would like you to meet."

"Thank you for thinking of me, Mildred," I replied. "I have a busy, full life with teenagers, a small business, and the need to help my elderly mother-in-law." Indeed, my last seventeen months were filled to overflowing with the challenging decisions of disposing of the Henry Lincks Contracting business.

Now, with it behind me and the girls soon heading off to college, I intended to finally finish my masters degree and pursue opportunities to teach abroad. I had no intention of dating.

But Mildred Gubany was hardly a woman easily discouraged. She always managed to find me on league day. For three months I listened to multitudes of accolades about this man, Jack Wulfmeyer:

"He is Vice President of Sales and Marketing for a large manufacturing company."

"Jack's position requires him to oversee the training of young sales trainees."

"It also includes lecturing and seeking potential businesses worldwide."

"He also drives a classy new Lincoln Continental Touring car."

If Mildred had known me well, she would have known *none* of it impressed me.

After three months, she was exasperated with my disinterest. Her last salvo was, "Well, Sue, this is your chance to go out with a good Christian man."

Her very last statement piqued my curiosity, but with caution. Was this man a Christian *in name only?* Did he have a personal relationship with Jesus? The Bible is very clear on this point. John 3 explains that we must be born again to have this relationship. 1 Corinthians 6:14 says, "Do not marry an unbeliever."

The question in my heart was, "Should I even go out with this man?" After talking to my girls, I agreed to one date.

Exactly one year and fifteen days following Howard's untimely departure from this earth, I came face-to-face with Mr. Jack Wulfmeyer as he knocked on my front door.

As I opened up the door, a handsome, immaculately dressed gentleman exclaimed, "Hi, I'm your blind date for the evening. My friends Paul and Mildred Gubany are waiting for us in their car!"

This was my first date since losing Howard. Mildred's persistence brought this evening to fruition. She, Paul, Jack, and I enjoyed dinner in one of my favorite places, Westport Village. This area in West St. Louis County was built to replicate a small European village. I turned to Jack, exclaiming, "Isn't this a charming place!"

He replied, "What's charming about it?"

I thought to myself, *I don't have anything in common with this man.* Even so, I *did* accept his following invitation for dinner.

He turned to me and asked, "May I pick you up for church next Sunday?" He was a member of Centenary Methodist church in downtown St. Louis, very close to his high rise apartment. Every Sunday thereafter he drove 45 miles *one way* to pick me up in Concord Village and then head back downtown to church.

My world quickly filled up with Cardinal baseball games, light operas in Forest Park, scrumptious Italian meals out, and exquisite bouquets of flowers delivered straight to my doorstep.

"The Hill" became our favorite dining place. It sat in the Italian section of St. Louis. At those dinners, I continually talked about Howie. On our fourth date together, I made up my mind to not mention Howie's name. But as the evening rolled along, suddenly I found myself doing it again!

"Oh, Jack, please forgive me," I pleaded. "You have to be sick of hearing about Howie."

But Jack reached across the table, took my hand, and solemnly responded, "Sue, it's obvious you need to talk about Howie. You go ahead and talk about him as long as you need to." It was that night when I began to admire his character in a new and refreshing way. His perception and sensitivity deeply touched my heart.

Pleasant evenings sitting on our upper patio became the location for us to deeply connect. We shared our lives. Jack was divorced after twenty-seven years of marriage. I was widowed after nineteen years of marriage. We discovered how similar the emotions connected with divorce and death actually were. We shared about our parenting challenges. Jack had young adult children, two sons and two daughters. He was learning to navigate rough waters as they emerged into adulthood. I listened to Jack's deep frustration with the president of his company.

Since Jill and Holly were still under my roof, they became acquainted with Jack as well. Because they had seen a similar situation with their grandparents experiencing loss and mourning followed by a healthy remarriage, my children were not resentful of Jack's presence in my life. And they welcomed him into their lives as well. In fact, Jill and Holly grew in their respect and trust for him.

One day, as I headed up our driveway after a long day working at Kimmswick, I was shocked to see Jack's car parked there. *What could possibly be going on?!?*

Walking in the house, there stood Jack and the girls grinning from ear to ear. The three looked like the proverbial cat that had swallowed the canary. I wondered what they were up to.

Suddenly, Jack's question last week flashed through

my mind. "Sue, what is that hole in your kitchen wall?" I whipped my head around to see my intercom system had been installed.

Instantly, I blurted out, "Oh no, Jack Wulfmeyer, you have been in my messy disorganized basement!"

He smiled broadly saying, "Yes, and I survived."

By this time I knew how organized and particular Jack Wulfmeyer was. Recovering from my shock and embarrassment, I shared, "Jack, I am thrilled to have my intercom installed. I can't thank you enough."

"The girls told me you would be," he replied with a wink.

Returning from dinner on a balmy summer evening, we took a walk in the moonlight. Jack stopped, took my hand, and told me he loved me. I had managed to keep Jack at arm's length until now. Taking a deep breath, I responded, "Jack, I think we should stop seeing each other."

Shock and sadness reverberated in his next words. "Sue, haven't we been having a good time together?"

"Well…, yes," I admitted.

"Then let's just keep enjoying each other's company," he responded.

"If you're sure you are content with our just being friends," I replied.

Jack and I, during our period of dating.

After that time, I often would return home from work to find Jill rolling her expressive big brown eyes, telling me in a dreamy voice, "I was just on the phone with Jack for *half an hour.*" It almost seemed as if *she* was the one falling in love with him!

But Jill would soon be out from my nest. She was in the midst of packing for college at New Mexico State University in Las Cruces, New Mexico. One of her dad's dying requests had been, "Jill, please go west for college. Your allergies will be less of a problem there." Holly and I were planning to drive her out in our little, two-door Chevy.

But Jack kept pestering me, "Let me drive you there in my car. It's so much larger."

I was dragging my feet. *How would that* appear *to people?* I wondered.

As if sensing my discomfort with the whole idea, the girls assured me, "Mom, *we'll* be with you and Jack. We're your chaperones." That convinced me to accept Jack's offer. Soon, we four were off to New Mexico. We planned to stay a few days to get Jill all settled in, and then return.

While we were there, Jill requested we have lunch together. She had something she wanted to discuss with us. As we sat enjoying each other's company while eating a tasty lunch, Jill abruptly turned to Jack.

"Jack, I want to know your intentions towards my mother," she declared.

I sat there horrified. My own daughter was bringing up a subject I had successfully avoided. At that very moment, I wished I could just disappear. And she continued,

"Specifically, when are you going to get married?"

Jack was grinning from ear to ear. Jill had succeeded in swinging open the door he had been so waiting for!

Following lunch, Jack suggested we return to the little Las Cruces church we had attended on Sunday. All of us wanted to examine their exquisite stained glass windows.

Sitting in a pew admiring the windows, Jack asked with an air of caution, "What did you think about Jill's proposal?"

I sat in silence for a long time. Sending up my often-used "arrow prayers," I began realizing what Jesus was showing me. I turned to Jack, now my best friend, and told him, very slowly, "I believe our Lord's plan is for us to be husband and wife." Once again, I saw my own career plans fading away.

In a flash, Jack was on the phone with his pastor. He had the wheels spinning fast for our wedding. After talking with his pastor by phone, Jack learned the only two dates available were October 21st – just six weeks away – or June 10th the following year.

We looked at each other and our thoughts matched: "Well, we're not getting any younger. October 21st it is!"

Driving back to St. Louis from Las Cruces, we wrote our wedding ceremony. We sent out our invitations to the immediate family. In the midst of this whirlwind, I developed cold feet.

"Jack, I just can't go through with this," I hedged. The last four years I had held dying loved ones in my arms. I didn't want to lose anyone else I loved. Jack's reaction was total silence. He told me later he knew all he could do was pray.

A week before the wedding, in my quiet time God's still voice whispered into my ear, "Are you a fraud? Didn't you turn your life over to me?" And more. "Have you forgotten Proverbs 3:5-6? *Trust in the Lord with all your heart and lean not on your own understanding. In all your ways acknowledge him and he will make your paths straight.*"

My immediate reaction was, "Oh Lord, forgive me! And, oh, Jack, please forgive me!"

Gathering our six children and one grandchild from New Mexico and Ohio, along with our immediate family members, Jack and I were united in marriage on October 21, 1977 at Centenary Methodist Church. We flew to Honolulu the next morning for a three-day electrical convention. Then our honeymoon started with a week on each of the two islands, Maui and Kauai.

What a start to a life of adventure! Even during this short stretch, we snorkeled with brilliantly colored fish and among packs of sea turtles. We then went on to try scuba diving; what a treat it was to watch manta rays feeding at night under brilliant lights. And the luaus! I can close my eyes even now and remember even the tiniest details.

This trip marked the beginning of fulfilling a lifelong dream to travel. As Jack and I grew as a couple, his heart's desire became to fulfill that dream together.

"Susie, we will explore faraway lands together. You just wait!"

Jack and I on our wedding day.

I loved snorkeling in Hawaii on our honeymoon!

Returning home from an idyllic two-week honeymoon in Hawaii, our next decision concerned our new home together. When I first met Jack, he was starting to work with a decorator. He was building a three-story condo in St. Louis County. He introduced me to his decorator, announcing, " I would like you to work with Sue." She and I decorated his new home right down to coordinating bath and tea towels.

Immediately I knew he thought we would live there. "Jack, I can't move into your new condo."

He was shocked. "But, Sue," he responded in disbelief, "you have decorated it so beautifully."

"Jack, I would love to move there. I really would," I confided. "But I can't enroll Holly in a new high school. This is her senior year. Can't you move into my home?"

A bit reluctantly, Jack understood my dilemma. The new Mr. and Mrs. Jack Wulfmeyer would reside at 10101 Courtwick Drive, St. Louis, Missouri, in my home. During the next two years, Jill, Holly, Jack, and I evolved into a close-knit family.

Yet Jack's dissatisfaction with his job continued.

Repeatedly at business seminars, he would hear, "If you are unhappy in your job, you should quit." It was a mystery to me why he could not see the many advantages and perks of his position. His gifts of organization and management seemed to me to be ideal for his position as Vice President of Sales and Marketing. His staff was full of talent, especially Cyril Cadwallader, his international man. Jack relished the challenges of appearing before the corporation. It appeared to me in due time he seemed destined to become President of the company.

In the fall of 1979, Jack sat in Columbia University's prestigious *Upper Management for Senior Executives* seminar. There, at the exquisite Harriman Estate in upstate New York, the speaker pointed right at him and said, "If you are unhappy in your job, you should quit!"

He called me that evening. I listened to the excitement in his voice as he related the day's events. My heart sank. I sensed what God's still small voice was saying. Upon Jack's return home he reiterated the message. Knowing Jack's discontent in his job, I felt God's prodding. I took a deep breath, and with all my resolve and strength uttered, "Well, it looks like the Lord is telling you to resign."

We prayed together for several days about this decision. I watched him literally soar as he headed out the door Monday morning. His feet never touched the ground. He was filled with a spirit of determination and elation.

But my feet? They just felt glued to the floor. I was dumbfounded and paralyzed at the thought of what he was about to do.

Gone would be those amazing trips abroad so perfectly orchestrated by Cyril.

The movies of our business trips flashed through my head.

No more personal chauffeur through England, or personal escorts and entertainment in Japan. I recalled how privileged I felt to have been entertained by a wealthy Japanese businessman and his wife. They spent twelve hours showing us elaborate shrines in Kyoto, dining together and giving us a royal feast in a private room while geisha girls danced for us.

To cap off that particular day, this Japanese businessman requested a banjo be brought to him. Then he sang *Deep In The Heart Of Texas* using the only English words he knew. Through our interpreter, we learned he had picked up this song from listening to American servicemen in post-WWII occupied Japan.

My mind flew off to Sydney and Melbourne, Australia, where company executives took us on a trip to the Outback. From one grove of eucalyptus trees, raucous laughter assaulted us as we ate lunch.

"What on earth is that?" I asked my guide.

"It's a kookaburra bird." Ah, the famed kookaburras of the old song I had sung around the campfire at Girl

Scout camp long ago: *"Kookaburras sit on the old gum tree, merry, merry king of the bush is he!! Laugh Kookaburra, laugh kookaburra, gay your life must be."*

It wasn't until this very moment this hilarious, joyful song made sense to me. Now I knew.

A ringing phone jolted me out of my fanciful recollections, now wrapped in sadness. On the other end, I heard an ecstatic voice ring out, "I'm free, I'm free! I gave my boss my resignation notice. He accepted it, and I am out of here!"

I could envision Jack's beaming smile and sparkling eyes right through the phone. I was filled with joy for him. A fleeting thought crossed my mind. I was also free of his boss' suspicious wife. She used me to check up on her husband's whereabouts. He and Jack traveled and held many business dinners together. She told me she suspected he was having an affair. He was. I refrained from divulging my knowledge of this sticky situation. My prayers and sympathy went out to her. Much later I learned this was not the first time he had been unfaithful.

This event catapulted us into one adventure after another for the next ten months. We met with our pastor Andy Jumper at our church, The Second Presbyterian Church of Clayton, Missouri.

"Pastor Jumper," we began, "we are interested in exploring mission possibilities." At the same time, we gave our tithe for the coming year while we still had the funds.

One evening, as we were praying and seeking direction, the phone rang. Picking it up, I was greeted with, "Susie, what are you kids going to do for the next few months? Why don't you head out to Mesa, Arizona and stay in our condo? Barb and I won't arrive until Christmas."

Some time after mother's death, my stepfather Martin had met and married a lovely Christian lady. Our whole family fell fast in love with Barbara and her blithe spirit.

Jack and I jumped at his generous offer. We hadn't found a missionary fit yet. The girls were both away at college. Holly was now attending the University of Missouri in Columbia. As new empty nesters, we were now "footloose and fancy free."

Telling our family and friends Jack had resigned as VP of Bussman *and* we were heading west brought on a flood of discouraging outbursts.

"You did what? Are you *out of your mind*?"

"You've just thrown away your future and all your security."

Jack, you're fifty, what kind of a job can you get?"

"You've just burned your bridges behind you."

My friends shook their heads. "Sue, you will never have a beautiful home again like the one Howard built for you."

Not discouraged by such remarks, we joyously looked forward to a snow- and ice-free winter basking in the warm Arizona sun. We set off on Highway 40, anticipating the adventures ahead. Within two days of our arrival, Jibby and Ruth Florin, resident snowbirds (the label locals gave winter residents), approached us by the pool.

"We hear you want to stay here after your family returns. We will make it worth your while if you will stay in our condo for the season."

Jack and I looked at each other in amazement. Did we hear them right? Could this really be happening? "Yes," was our unflinching reply. With that, our two months morphed into five months of life-changing events, filled with surprises at every turn.

The pleasant, sun-drenched desert winter weather of Arizona made tennis games, swimming, golf and hunting a daily affair. Upon arrival, locals told us the picturesque sunburnt-red mountains were a mere fifteen minutes away.

We jumped into the car and headed for the mountains our very first evening in Mesa.

The spectacular desert sunset over Phoenix and the Salt River as well as the reflection of the spectrum of evening hues took our breath away. Sitting together watching the sunset soon became one of our nightly rituals.

Top on our agenda in Mesa, Arizona was looking for a church and a job. We visited a Presbyterian church. The

I had plenty of time to up my game during our stay in beautiful Mesa.

following Sunday it was a Methodist church. Being gainfully unemployed, we needed to be frugal. Jack suggested, "Let's check out the Baptist church close to us. We can walk to it and save gas."

I added, "We can keep in shape, too!"

Neither one of us had ever attended a Baptist church. All we knew about their guidelines were that they didn't allow dancing, card games, or lipstick (for women). Those rules certainly had not been a part of our church experience. Nevertheless, we decided to attend.

As we walked in the door, the members greeted us warmly. When the service ended, the couple behind us introduced themselves and, to our surprise, invited us to their home for dinner. As we continued to chat, the pastor came over to greet us. He smiled, remarking, "You two don't look like snow birds!"

Jack replied without missing a beat. " No we're not. We are looking for job opportunities."

At that, the pastor offered, "Meet me Wednesday at 2pm in my office. I think I can help you."

We came to realize our impression of Baptist legalism was completely off base. The Holy Spirit seemed alive and well in that place. We knew we had found our church.

"Sunset gazing time!" Jack called out our second night in Mesa. The minute our feet touched the desert floor, we looked up and saw quail. With their top knots bobbing in the desert grass, they were everywhere. While I admired their rich color and amusing antics, Jack instead imagined the incredible quail hunting potential right there.

The very next morning Jack exclaimed, "Susie, let's go skeet shooting!" I agreed to go, thinking to myself, *he's in for a big surprise*.

Taking our place in the shooting box, Jack handed me a gun. I immediately started the hunters ritual of checking it out. Jack stood watching me, utterly shocked. "Whoa, Susie! You sure know how to handle a gun!"

He yelled, "Pull," and I hit the first clay bird right out of the chute. We both were shocked. I hadn't shot a gun since I was a little girl. I told Jack how my Uncle Clarence taught us as young kids to handle a gun properly. My cousin Howard Junior and I had a friendly rivalry trying to beat each other in target practice.

Jack could hardly believe his good fortune. "Susie, we can hunt together!" he exclaimed.

"Jack, I will be delighted to hunt with you," I responded. "While you shoot with your gun, I will shoot with my camera. I can't shoot those exquisite little quail."

He was disappointed, but he understood. I will admit, however, I did enjoy feasting on those delicious delicacies he shot.

In our five months in Arizona we had many great adventures hunting together. One time, we were walking in the mountains, but it felt as if someone was following us. Turning around ever so slowly, we stood there in disbelief. A herd of wild horses had been tracking us. But the minute we gasped, they fled in fright. We also encountered rattlesnakes and Javelina wild pigs out there in the desert.

One day before Christmas we had just finished

I frequently enjoyed the beautiful desert scenery during our time in Mesa.

Jack, hunting in Mesa.

hunting. I sat watching Jack dress the quail he had just shot. Suddenly, three large Canadian geese flew very low right over our heads.

"Jack, quick, shoot one! We can have Christmas goose for dinner!" I exclaimed.

"Susie, I can't get a direct shot. I never want to just wound a bird." I was disappointed – no goose – and full of admiration – he cared about those birds . As we headed home, three distinct shots rang out in the distance. "Oh, oh, someone is in trouble. Hunters are only allocated two geese," Jack remarked.

Soon, along came a pickup truck. The driver waved at us, inquiring, "Would you like a goose? I have to dispose of one before the game warden catches me."

I was amazed. "Jack, all my life I have dreamed of having goose for Christmas dinner," I shared.

Jack responded, "We'll take it." He knew exactly how to dress and prepare the bird for cooking.

That year, three of our four daughters joined us for Christmas. Jack's daughter Cindy came from Santa Fe, New Mexico. Holly, now at the University of Missouri, flew in from Columbia, Missouri, and Jill, studying at New Mexico State University in Las Cruces, joined us. And what did we eat? Christmas goose with all the trimmings. It was truly grand!

In February, First Baptist Church invited missionaries on furlough to share their experiences with the congregation. We were able to invite one of the young couples, Dan and Wendy Sherman, to our place for dinner. The Shermans were on sabbatical from their post in Malawi, Africa. We had planned for a two-hour dinner, but that morphed into six! We connected so well!

The Shermans served with Campus Crusade for Christ. At that time, Jack and I knew little about that organization. "Jack and Sue, you've got to visit Arrowhead Springs, our headquarters in San Bernardino, California," they insisted. "You can meet Bill Bright, Campus Crusade's founder, when you come. We can make all the arrangements." Indeed, their enthusiasm and glowing description of the Campus Crusade ministry proved contagious.

Since we had already set business appointments to investigate career opportunities in Northern California, dropping by Arrowhead Springs in the San Bernardino mountains was actually right on the way. So we made a plan, and soon the day arrived.

We were taken aback by Campus Crusade for Christ's stunning campus. We learned it had been a resort retreat for Hollywood stars before the advent of flying.

Our guided tour of the campus took us to a serene chapel, a lively natural hot springs and a spectacular swimming pool. Our guide told us, "This is the pool built for the Esther Williams' swimming movies."

At that, I gasped in delight and blurted out, "She was my inspiration for swimming and diving in my youth. I saw all her movies!"

Later, when we met with Bill Bright, he quickly perceived Jack's gifts, talents, and management skills. After some time together, he inquired, "Would you pray and consider becoming part of my staff?"

We were honored to be asked. We filled out the required extensive background application form, but made it clear our decision would come through prayer. Bill invited us to attend their summer training session to learn more about the ministry. We gladly accepted.

Our northern California business appointments completed, we decided to stop at Campus Crusade headquarters on our way home. We got to spend more time with Bill, his wife Vonette, and Stephen Douglas, Bill's assistant. Stephen and Jack were the same age; both held degrees in engineering and MBAs. Jack and I were like two sponges soaking up rich Christian fellowship while learning more about the organization.

Picking up the newspaper when we arrived back in Mesa, we discovered the National Electrical Convention was underway at the luxurious resort of Mountain Shadows in Scottsdale, Arizona. We knew so many people in that organization, we decided to drop in.

As we sat by the pool chatting with friends, Bob

Pinero, president of a major manufacturing company, walked by and recognized Jack. He shot two quick questions at Jack. "What are *you* doing here?" and, "Have you severed all ties with your former company?"

"As a matter of fact, yes I have," Jack replied.

Immediately, Bob suggested, "The two of you, meet me in my suite in fifteen minutes. Let's talk." We soon found ourselves sitting in Bob's suite, listening to him offer Jack three different positions in his company. Jack informed him we had planned an extensive trip to Europe, so it would be impossible to start any job before September.

"No problem!" was Bob's reply.

Driving back to St. Louis, we had time to discuss and pray for direction with both these opportunities.

Arriving back in St. Louis from Arizona, we engaged a realtor to sell our home. Then we packed for our seven-week trip to Europe. Feeling quite breezy and carefree, we bid our family and friends goodbye.

Now we were off to Europe! A spirit of pure adventure flooded our minds as we flew to Copenhagen, Denmark on May 15, 1980. Armed with our Bibles and four travel books, our roundtrip tickets, a two-week Eurail pass, a car reserved in Frankfort, and our first night's lodging set, we were flying high – both literally and figuratively.

Fresh springs of anticipation had filled us as we pored over Fodor's *Guide to Europe, Let's Go Europe, Europe on Fifteen Dollars a Day*, and *Waldo's European Travel Book* in the lead-up to this trip. Fodor's led us to fabulous bed and breakfasts; *Europe on Fifteen Dollars a Day*, aimed at student travelers, catered to our frugal ambitions. Its tip on finding a full, free breakfast in the Oslo Train Station fed us for an entire day! And we relied on Myra Waldo's book for special splurge days. We found one of her *not to miss tips*, telling us of Franz Joseph's favorite Konditori and the Sacher Torte at the Sacher Hotel in Vienna, to be pure ambrosia.

Hydrofoils, trains, boats and ferries took us through Denmark, Sweden, Norway and down the Rhine River. The castles rising high above the Rhine beckoned to us from our ferry.

"Jack, let's jump off the ferry here! Maybe we can stay in that castle high on the mountain side," I begged. We headed straight for the pharmacy in the quaint village with its cobblestone streets. Our research taught us European pharmacists were required to speak English so they could help tourists. Sure enough, the pharmacist welcomed us and arranged for our castle overnight in the turret room. Back in its heyday, the builders had perfectly designed its narrow vertical windows to patrol the Rhine River.

Experience had taught us few people spoke English in the villages. When we saw school children, we knew they were studying English. In our limited German, we greeted them with *Guten Morgen, Sprichst du Englisch?* The many personal interactions we were able to enjoy with Europeans along the way enriched our cultural understanding by leaps and bounds.

Driving through Germany, Austria and Switzerland, we stayed in bed and breakfasts. To our surprise, we learned it was only the English who stayed in B&Bs. Other Europeans didn't do that. And most Americans at the time opted for big fancy hotels. Remember, this was 1980.

We would immediately tell our prospective hosts we were Americans. Their first reaction was one of shock. Then excitement. They were actually having *Americans* in their home! If we stayed in a B&B winery, the hosts always showered us with their wine.

We packed many maps and photos of the U.S. to give out as gifts. These made unique and easy-to-transport gifts. Mornings when we were anxious to be off on our next day's adventure, invariably our hosts just didn't want us to leave. They eagerly poured over maps with us. With our meager grasp of the German language and often theirs of English, examining the maps together was a saving grace, allowing us to communicate and build our friendship.

Zooming down the famous German Salt Mines was one item on our bucket list. We selected a B&B on the border of Germany and Austria. Arriving the next morning at the Salt Mine, we donned the requisite white attire. A small tram waited for us to climb in. Instantly, it jettisoned us down a dark tunnel. Screeching to a halt, we found ourselves in a white world of salt. Wow! It was an unusual and exhilarating experience! We learned this particular salt mine had been used by the Germans to store and protect famous works of art during WWII.

Hiking the Alps was a dream I had held since childhood. I was enthralled when I read the book *Heidi*. And then the film *Sound of Music* set my desire on fire. Now, spread out right before me in all their grandeur, those picturesque Alpine scenes were becoming a reality!

The Visitor's Center at the German-Austrian border offered a small booklet in German about a prehistoric ice cave. At the time, we couldn't find any information in English. So we relied on the German book, straining to grasp enough ideas as we drove across the border to catch the Austrian lift.

As we exited the lift into the brilliant June day, we discovered a walking path, complete with steps carved through the mountain as we climbed. Then, emerging from the dark mountain, a steep snow-covered climb to the cave entrance greeted us. There stood the ever-present, uniformed German money collector. We seemed to see a version of him wherever we went, be it high in the Alps or standing sentry at the ubiquitous public toilets. Two young German couples were waiting to tour the cave as well. Our helpful money collector served as our guide. Entering the dark ice cave, he lit magnesium strips to give us brilliant light. When the strips burned out, we found ourselves pitched into gaping darkness.

After our ice-cave adventure, I admitted to Jack, "I'm not sure I can physically hike all the way back to the lift." The two German couples pointed to an extremely narrow snow-and-ice-covered path. Listening to their conversation,

I thought I recognized the expression for "more dangerous." I sent up a prayer and then suggested, "Jack, let's follow them."

The young couples speeding ahead soon disappeared from our sight. It was such a harrowing experience, inching along the sheer ice field, knowing one slip would plunge us straight down the mountainside. Finally, we came upon a charming wooden hut. This one sported a sign in the front reading, "Tony Linz's Hut." I learned later about the many such huts designated for hikers, each with different names, were scattered throughout the Alps.

Staggering through the door, we came upon the young German couples. The warm, cozy hut and their smiling faces beckoned us to join them. We felt as if God had wrapped his loving arms around us at just that moment. We were safe.

These new German friends motioned to us to join them. They passed the pitcher they were circulating among them and invited us to partake. That was my first ever communal drink, and it meant so much to me. When I sipped from it, I was startled at the taste of beer mixed with lemonade – a combination I had never expected. But for us, it was a cup of gratitude.

Completing our bowls of hot soup, we were ready to head down the mountain. We trod along wooden steps alternating with landings for us to rest all the way down to the base of the mountain. The young couples became concerned about us and started waiting until we appeared. Attempting to communicate, one couple started speaking some English words. We learned the girl's father was an American soldier and her boyfriend had taken two years of English in high school.

As we reached the bottom of the mountain with weary, aching bones, Helmut, Rosie and their friends were waiting for us. Helmut informed Jack he had a problem.

"Your car is parked in Austria and you are now in Germany."

In the 1980's, there were checkpoints at every border crossing in Europe. Helmut continued on, telling us he had a plan.

"We'll take you to get your car. Jack, you sit in the back seat of our car. And don't say a word!" The border guard would be suspicious of two Germans together with an American. I waited with the two girls until the men's safe return. Later, Helmut and Rosie took us to their favorite restaurant nearby, and we had a delightful evening together. We corresponded for several years.

Entering the Bavarian area of Germany, we discovered this was the year of the Oberammergau Passion Play. Excitedly, I turned to Jack. "I have dreamed of seeing this play since fourth grade. Our teacher taught us about its history."

The Passion Play arose under these circumstances: The plague was raging in Europe in 1633. The villagers of Oberammergau promised God they would perform live the suffering, death and resurrection of Jesus Christ every tenth year in a plea for no further plague deaths. Since 1634, the Passion Play the villagers of Oberammergau have been performing this play every ten years.

Rushing to the ticket office, we discovered the only way to purchase a ticket was lining up at dawn in hopes someone would turn in their ticket, making it available for us to buy. Early the next morning in the shivering cold, Jack and I took turns standing in line while the other could warm up in the car.

I was next in line at the box office at 9:00 am, when the six-hour play started. At that moment, I spied someone walking into the box office. The hefty German man behind me spotted that person, too. *Could it be they might have two tickets*? I wondered in anticipation, throwing up a prayer in the process.

Yes, they had turned in two tickets! That German man shoved me pretty hard to get his hands on the tickets. But the German crowd surrounding us shouted to the ticket agent, "This lady is next!" Gratitude and admiration filled my heart for these people. Thanks to these people, who had defended a foreigner, we sat in the eighth row center to witness a live enactment of The Passion of Christ. It was one of the most moving experiences of my life.

Flying home, we felt like millionaires, so enriched by friendships forged, European culture, magnificent scenery, and extraordinary experiences.

Arriving back in St. Louis, we made plans to visit family in Illinois and Ohio before heading for Fort Collins, Colorado. We had accepted Campus Crusade's invitation to attend their summer training conference.

The conference burst with enthusiasm and vitality. The outstanding evangelical Christian speakers and Christian musicians both impressed and inspired. We attended mostly executive ministry training sessions.

Returning to our dorm room one night, we questioned ourselves. *Could we be evangelists? What, exactly, did that even mean?* That concept was never in our Methodist and Presbyterian backgrounds. Still, we felt a strong pull to the spiritual energy and joy we found there.

We prayed together and following an especially moving evening, Jack turned to me. "Susie," he proclaimed, "I believe I can be more effective spreading God's word by accepting Gould Shawmut's offer as an electrical manufacturer's representative in Northern California and Nevada. By becoming one of their independent reps, we can dedicate the business to the ministry. We can also train young people on how a Christian business actually works."

Admittedly, I did have a pang in my heart. I thought what a privilege and spiritually enriching experience it would be to work with Bill and Vonette at Campus Crusade headquarters. At the same time, I knew the depth of Jack's entrepreneurial spirit and his business acumen. His heart for Jesus reassured me. I embraced this decision.

Our ten months of being "gainfully unemployed" were cataclysmic and life-changing, physically and

Though Jack had decided to pursue work as an electrical manufacturer's representative, our involvement with Campus Crusade continued over several decades as we supported their mission.

spiritually. Some might label our ten months of adventure a mystery for its unexpected twists and turns. We believe it was all part of a master plan.

Jack's decision was inspired. Our next 38 years in California proved fantastic. Doors flung wide open for ministry and training young people. We also could support various Campus Crusade ministries.

Opening the mail one day early on, our eyes popped. It was a special business bonus! Jack and I looked at each other with identical thoughts in our minds. *Let's donate this to Campus Crusade! We have a roof over our head and food on our shelves – what more do we need!* We had no idea this decision would lead us into being one of the founders of Campus Crusade's Trinity College. That school was established – and still remains – in the Empire State building today.

Our relationship with Bill and Vonette Bright grew. We attended their 50th wedding anniversary celebration. We got to lead the efforts to premiere Campus Crusade's production of *America, You're Too Young To Die* in Northern California.

Bill purchased the rights to the movie produced by Warner Brothers entitled, *The Jesus Story*. Jack immediately told him, "Bill, we want a copy of that film!"

"Sorry Jack," Bill responded, "I only have five copies." We persisted. Mysteriously, some unknown person placed one in our hands. Was it an angel?

Have you seen *The Jesus Story?* Our life has been filled with the joy of distributing this life-changing film worldwide since 1983. Jack's words uttered at the Campus

Crusade summer conference were prophetic. Our move to California served as the springboard for the spreading of the gospel of love and hope to the world.

8

Golden Hills, Golden Dreams

Poppies

Symbolizing success, love, beauty, and eternal life

I didn't waste any time to say goodbye to St. Louis' hot, humid summers and snowy, frigid winters. That part was easy.

But saying goodbye to Holly at the University of Missouri proved rather tough. Still, our excitement at what lay ahead overshadowed our sadness at leaving family and friends behind.

The golden hills of California magically kept beckoning Jack. Memories of the three colorful years he had spent there in the early 1960s still danced in his mind. Now, 17 years later, Jack was bringing me to his beloved Walnut Creek, California. Anticipation filled my heart.

With a sense of relief, we finally arrived on September 15, 1980. A fountain, with a giant globe at its center, greeted us; what a perfect introduction for our new adventure! We pulled up to the gate of Rossmoor, the retirement community we would now call home. Jack was just over 50, but that qualified him to move into this place as the owners had recently – and only for a short time – lowered the age.

Being right around 50 and moving into a gated retirement community may seem a bit odd. But the reason we made this choice is because we knew we'd be on the road a lot for the business. We wanted a place we could feel comfortable leaving for long stretches. This type of community would cover security and maintenance for us while away. We had prayed about this, and this was the vision God had placed upon our hearts.

The guard welcomed us to the gated community and offered clear directions to our rented condo.

We were, indeed, two weary travelers! Our 2000-mile trek across half the United States was now at an end. We had driven two packed vehicles in tandem across those many miles. Jack, in the lead, drove his Ford van, while I followed him driving his large Lincoln Town Car.

The moment we arrived, Jack sprang into action. Unlocking the door to the condo, Jack told me, "Susie, just relax awhile. We will unpack after I set up an answering service. Headquarters expects us to be open for business today!" Those were welcome words.

A few days later, our business set in motion and our unpacking done, we could catch our breath. Jack, always sensitive to the blitz of change he had brought to my life, then asked me, "Honey, what will you do?"

My immediate response was, "I will fulfill one of my heart's desires. I will attend Bible Study Fellowship!"

Bible Study Fellowship, or BSF, began through the efforts of a former missionary, Miss Johnson, at Carmel Presbyterian Church in Carmel, California in 1969. The BSF approach to Bible Study quickly spread across the United States and abroad. Since first hearing about this excellent in-depth Bible-based study, I had yearned to attend it. Now was God's perfect timing, and I was overjoyed. It was the ideal segue from St. Louis to the metropolitan area of San Francisco. Now my circle of friendship was about to greatly expand.

Our Rossmoor condo backed up to the Las Trampas mountain range. We could literally walk out our door and hike all over that fantastic mountain range. Many evenings we whipped up a quick dinner, put it in our backpacks, and enjoyed a tasty (and romantic) sunset picnic on a mountain top.

Our encounter with the region's wildlife was thrilling, and occasionally hair-raising. On the trail, we would run into numerous coastal deer, signs and sounds of cougars, and a wide range of snakes, including rattlers and huge

The Rossmoor condos, right next to the Las Trampas mountains.

Tigger, our first pet.

tarantulas. One evening we discovered a tiny, abandoned feral kitten.

"Oh, Jack," I pleaded, "We can't leave it to die! But I know you don't like cats."

"You are such an animal lover, Susie. Pick it up, and we'll take it to the condo."

Once tamed, he grew into our beloved "Tigger" cat, our first pet.

I could have never imagined my life in California would become so fulfilling. I had become the public relations arm for Jack's company, G & R Sales, a manufacturer's representative organization. Donning my chauffeur's cap, I drove Jack around northern California and Nevada. This allowed him time to study and familiarize himself with the new territory, and specifically the companies he would be calling on. While he met with potential clients, I delighted in the time to delve deeply into my Bible study.

When Jack presented his business card to new customers in California, they were instantly curious. Many inquired about the unusual name for our company, G & R Sales. Customarily in California people used their name or initials in the manufacturer's representative business. We chose this name because of Jack's long history with G & R, the very first company he had worked for as a 20 year-old.

Gene Stossberg and Robert "Bob" Rodenroth, two entrepreneurial engineers, founded G & R in the late 1940s as an electrical repair business mainly dealing with radios. When Gene joined another business, Robert quickly realized the company's need for an electrical engineer. A new and exciting invention was emerging, television. Jack, fresh out of college as of June 10, 1948 with his electrical engineering degree at a mere 20 years old, proved an ideal fit for G & R's expanding business.

Possessing an entrepreneurial spirit, Jack had turned down an invitation to train at IBM, now an established venture almost 40 years old. Instead, he jumped on the G & R Engineering ship. In the ensuing years, they continued to repair radios, fix televisions, install television antennas and develop the latest in hi-fi sound systems of the 1950s.

One day, Jack and Bob looked at each other and Jack suggested, "Maybe we oughtta get a real job. I mean, it's pretty fun, for sure. But it's not completely covering the bills."

So Jack and Bob each sought out more stable jobs. Both accepted positions with Emerson Electric in St. Louis while moonlighting to develop their G & R Engineering business on the side. Almost simultaneously they were both offered very attractive jobs. Bob left for a position in Warner Robbins, Georgia. White-Rodgers, a subsidiary of Emerson, recognizing Jack's gift of organization along with his electrical design expertise, offered him a job as a design engineer. They dissolved their partnership in G & R Sales, agreeing Jack would continue holding their business license.

Going to work for White-Rodgers, Jack never dreamed at the tender age of 27 he would become the foreman of their new building project. Upon its completion, Jack's entrepreneurial spirit kept nudging him and he sought out other job opportunities.

Jack's education, experience, and integrity, along with his commitment to excellence, attracted interest from several companies. He accepted a job at Greenleaf Manufacturing, creating electrical applications for their design engineer. This eventually lead to a position with Systron Donner in Walnut Creek, California. There, he designed gyroscopes for military use and accelerometers for missiles. At the same time, he was raising four children and acquiring an MBA in finance at UC Berkeley. Throughout his career, Jack continued to carry the G & R business license.

Now in Walnut Creek, California, Jack reactivated the G & R Sales business license in 1980. As the sole proprietor of this new season of G & R Sales, Jack was eager to "employ" me as his unpaid partner in the venture.

We dedicated this business to carrying out God's work through training young people in sales and marketing. Quarterly we sent out newsletters with a Christian message to all of our 240 customers in Northern California and Nevada.

We found the thrill and challenge of starting a new business both gratifying and, at times, discouraging. The first two years proved our most difficult. Often, the laid-back business culture in California made us feel as if we were in a foreign land.

We encountered this "foreignness" early one morning as we headed for San Francisco. Jack had put together a training program for an electric company. It wasn't easy back then to navigate the unfamiliar streets – no GPS systems, Google Maps, or the like. This, together with traffic, made arriving at the scheduled time no easy feat. Still, we made it! Jack collected his training materials and headed to the door. I settled into my Bible study in the car.

Suddenly, he rapped on the window. His quick return surprised me. Opening the car door, Jack exclaimed in consternation, "Their door is locked and no one is around!" We waited for awhile, but nobody came. Jack tucked his business card into the door with a personal note.

Not hearing from them, he called the next day. The business owner responded casually, "Oh we were just running late that day." This lax attitude miffed us at first. Sometimes we just felt like shutting down the business and returning to St. Louis!

A message in our *Closer Walk* Christian devotional one morning set us straight. The Apostle Paul, the writer of the Book of Philippians in the New Testament, instructs us to *"Forget the past and press on for what lies ahead."* (Philippians 3:13-14) Likewise, Luke in his Gospel admonishes us, *"If we have put our hand to the plow [work] and then look back, we are not fit for the kingdom of heaven."* (Luke 9:62)

Those compelling words propelled us ahead. In fact, we clung to them with everything we had. And, in time, we began to see the blessings in persevering.

One of those was regional travel. Since our business customers spanned Northern California and Nevada, we were able to enjoy so many opportunities to explore new territory. We scheduled a monthly trek north to the Oregon border, and then west to Redding, California.

These trips offered us breathtaking vistas of magnificent beauty: Northern California's towering redwood forests, giant sequoias and the crystal-clear Trinity River backdropped by the Trinity Alps, as we approached Redding. Just a bit further north, we would gaze in awe as Mount Shasta's majestic snow-capped peaks burst into view. These were among the countless extraordinary sights we could enjoy on our extended business trips together.

Along the way, we stayed at the historic Benbow Inn in Garberville, California. Built in 1926 by the architect Albert Farr, this early twentieth-century English-style inn quickly gained a following with a host of celebrities. These included First Lady Eleanor Roosevelt and U.S. Senator Herbert Hoover. Many movie stars used it as a retreat: Spencer Tracy, Clark Gable and Charles Laughton were among the movie greats who frequented the grounds. In fact, Charles Laughton stayed there while learning his lines for the original movie, *Mutiny on the Bounty*.

We enjoyed classic movies shown nightly in the Benbow Inn's own theater, something quite unusual at the

Jack and I with a completed puzzle in the Benbow Inn's common area on one of our many visits.

time. The crackling fire in the immense fieldstone fireplace beckoned us to relax in its glow, sinking into the sumptuous nearby chairs. Meanwhile, the proprietor offered aromatic English tea and fresh-out-of-the-oven scones; I can still taste their homemade lemon curd and clotted cream. Teatime at 4:00 pm every day meant a stream of delicacies on shiny silver trays parading before us.

On several tables in the common area, puzzles beckoned us to complete them. Jack and I soon discovered we both delighted in the challenge and camaraderie of the activity. Mouthwatering aromas filled the colossal glass-paned, solarium-style dining room, inviting us to lengthen our stay an extra day or two. When we did, we'd add hiking in the giant Redwoods and golfing to our business trek.

Eureka, California would be our next stop. The *Wall Street Journal* ran a tantalizing feature article on the Carter House B&B, so we decided to check it out. We were not disappointed with what we found.

Mark Carter, an entrepreneur, had unearthed architectural plans of a mansion destroyed in the San Francisco earthquake of 1906. The architects of that building also had crafted the world-renowned, Victorian-style Carson Mansion in Eureka. Using the original design plans, Mark and his hand-picked crew of three built the four-story structure in Eureka to match the former mansion's glory, handcrafting the intricate details on the wood wainscoting and mouldings.

Mark and his wife, Christi, a French gourmet cook, offered a delicate tart with a ground-almond filling, topped with thinly sliced apples, as one of their breakfast specialties. Fresh-squeezed orange juice, Eggs Florentine, Eggs Benedict, or a smoked salmon platter often accompanied the tart. Alongside came a fresh fruit compote overflowing with kiwi and raspberries or zabaglione and strawberries. And then there was the piping hot coffee or tea, constantly replenished.

The proprietors served wine and hors d'oeuvres promptly at 6 pm in the living room by the fire. During that time, we could enjoy such a relaxed and pleasurable time, connecting with fellow travelers. Liquors and sweets filled the buffet each evening. The entry hall always boasted a barrel brimming over with shiny red apples.

In the early 1980s, a chauffeured 1958 Bentley met all guests arriving by plane at the modest local airport. We were one of their first guests. Being monthly visitors, we were able to rejoice with Mark and Christi as they added a son and daughter to their nest. Today, there is an additional Carter Hotel across the street.

Our business trips also took us through the breathtaking vistas of Donner Pass. We marvelled at this scenic display of God's handiwork, enroute to Reno, Nevada. The glorious views of today belied the tragic history of its past. For a group of American pioneers, enroute from Independence, Missouri to California via wagon train in May 1846 ran into inclement and eventually fatal weather conditions crossing the summit. Delayed by a series of mishaps and mistakes, the group spent the winter of 1846–47 snowbound in the Sierra Nevada. Only 45 of the original

81 settlers survived.

Now, for us more than 100 years later, the summit's brilliant fall foliage and winter snow proved a tonic for our souls, enlivening our memories of the Midwest's seasons. Our experience of driving in ice and snow helped us navigate the winter road conditions. We would cover that winter trip with piles of extra prayers as we often found ourselves slipping and sliding into Reno.

In time, we found our in-home office bursting at the seams. We learned of another manufacturer's representative looking to share his office space in Concord, California, an ideal location for us living just next door in Walnut Creek. When he and Jack met, they both immediately realized the benefits of sharing office space and quickly drew up an agreement to do just that!

Moving into this office meant I had a new title, "Office Assistant." Years earlier, I would often work in my stepfather's law office during high school when his secretary, Ethel, took her summer vacation. That's when I learned just how much I disliked being cooped up in an office. This new job was definitely a labor of love!

Happily – and thankfully – we soon realized we needed another employee. We started interviewing young people for the position. In the middle of interviewing a

Jill and Jack with Jill's award for Outstanding Salesperson in the San Francisco Bay Area.

Holly and I at Holly's graduation from the University of Missouri in 1984.

promising young man, we received a surprise phone call from my daughter, Jill. With her diploma in hand from New Mexico State University, she was looking for a job.

"Jack, I would like to come to work for G & R Sales," Jill declared.

Oh, no! I instantly reacted. *Not* another *family business!*

But with my next thought, I realized *this* family business would have little resemblance to the anguish connected with the Henry Lincks' family contracting business. Euphoria filled my heart. I was elated to have my daughter with us; plus my office-assistant services would no longer be needed.

We founded and established our G & R Sales company on the solid rock of Christian principles. Jill realized she would receive excellent training for inside sales from Jack. With knowledge gained from growing up in a family business, this would prove a great asset for her budding career. Jill, with her innate gift of negotiation, convinced Jack he needed to pay for her move to California.

Jack took seriously his job of teaching Jill everything he knew about inside sales. This gave me double joy. I no longer had to do office work. *And* I had the pleasure of watching my daughter mature.

Then came the day Jack announced, "Jill, now you are ready for outside sales!"

With trepidation, she accepted his challenge. She soon discovered she was gifted in this arena. In fact, she ended up making history as the first female ever to receive the coveted award, "Outstanding Salesperson in the San

Holly's bridal shower.

Jill's bridal shower.

Francisco Bay Area!"

Jill never dreamed she would meet the love of her life, Jim Jacobs, in California. Jack took Jim under his wing, teaching him to demonstrate one of our electrical products. The rest is history; today Jill and Jim own our manufacturing representative's business, now called Century Sales.

One summer during her college years, Holly begged to come out to California to be with us. Well, she wanted to be with us, but *not* in a gated retirement community! We promised we'd find her a work arrangement where she could be with other young people. This turned out to be a political campaign, and it was there she met Chris Jones, a bright UC Berkeley Political Science student.

Their relationship stuck. Upon graduating Summa Cum Laude from the University of Missouri in 1984 with a degree in physical therapy, Holly decided to join us. And Chris, of course.

Turns out, those California golden hills beckoned both our girls. I was ecstatic. Now my girls and I were together again!

The toll of wedding bells ushered in the year 1986. First, Holly tied the knot with Chris on a sparkling July day. Just a few months later, Jill wed Jim on a sunny but breezy October day.

Holly and I on her wedding day.

Jill and I on her wedding day.

One might say we were once again empty nesters! But it was an interesting season, as we were now blessed with both couples living near us. In many ways, we felt our nest was now so full, our branches bent in family love.

We have been blessed time and again by our two sons-in-love, as we call them. After all, didn't they join our family through love?

With Jill now firmly established in sales for G & R, the door opened wide to us for new opportunities to travel, not only for business but also for fun! Indeed, my world would expand once again, this time in so many unexpected ways.

9

Traveling Life

Stephanotis

Symbolizing happiness in marriage and desire to travel.

The travel bug to explore faraway lands worked its way into my life when I was a mere five years old. I'd jump, clapping my hands, when my grandparents told me I could spend the day with my father's parents. They were welcoming home my globetrotting Uncle Herbert. I would sit enraptured at his feet as he told of his traveling adventures in Japan in the early 1900s.

Christened Herbert Pearlie Gray, my oldest uncle on my father's side was born in 1900. Bidding his family goodbye at 18, Uncle Herbert left farm life to see the world. Hitchhiking to California, he signed on as a crew member aboard a ship heading for Japan, a nation still closed to the outside world.

For many months after hopping off that Japan-bound freighter, he roamed the country. He learned of their culture of warlords and samurais. He told me about Nara, with its now world-renowned monkey statues, *Mizaru*, *Kikazaru* and *Iwazaru*, conveying their famous teaching, "See no evil, hear no evil and speak no evil." Uncle Herbert painted with words the austere beauty of the temples and gardens of Kyoto. He also raved about the stunning presence of Mount Fuji, Japan's national symbol of pride and elegance.

Even as a child, I thought to myself, "I want to go see those places!"

Through the years my uncle continued to entrance me with his adventure-filled life. As a teenager, I eagerly listened to his experiences living in Sumatra, Indonesia. He was in charge of Standard Oil of California there. He and his wife Maurie intrigued me with stories of the life on the island. The company furnished them a spacious home. It seemed servants took care of their every need. The only requirement imposed upon them was to always keep a barrel full of rice to pay the servants daily.

The jungle and its inhabitants fascinated them, even the geckos always scampering on their walls and ceilings. Life seemed full of adventure. In 1939, Maurie made history.

She was the first white woman to ever explore the depths of the Sumatran jungle. I idolized her adventurous spirit and yearned to experience it in my own life.

But suddenly their idyllic life abruptly ended. The Japanese bombed Pearl Harbor. Orders immediately came from Standard Oil to evacuate Maurie. She sailed out of the harbor bound for the U.S. the very next day. My uncle had orders to shut down the company and then return home. It took a year before they were reunited.

Their last great adventure took them to Maracaibo, Venezuela after World War II. Hearing about their life there led me to sign a letter of intent to teach school in Venezuela.

But then, of course, my marriage to Howard Lincks changed my direction. Nevertheless, the seed had been planted. I never lost my desire for travel.

Northward to the Land of the Midnight Sun

Our first journey for pleasure since our adventures around Europe took us up north to Alaska! Indeed, it was one of the places Jack had high on his bucket list. We researched and laid out our itinerary with great anticipation.

Presenting our plans to the Rossmoor Travel Agency, they then made all our travel reservations. Flying to Vancouver, Washington, we boarded a cruise ship bound for Juneau and Anchorage. The sight of orcas, their black and white bodies cavorting alongside our ship as it cut through the Pacific Ocean, took my breath away.

We found the Tlingit and Haida Indian lore in Ketchikan and Juneau fascinating. Their exquisitely carved, vividly colored totem poles reflected their love of the nature around them. We could not help but think this was their way to reaching out to a higher being.

Flying to Fairbanks, we joined a small tour group to hike and camp in Denali Park. They furnished us with white tents. I turned to Jack and inquired, "Why don't they furnish us with black tents?" Our tent proved to be so bright, making it difficult to sleep, since Alaska's midnight sun made it bright enough to read at 3 am!

Moose, bighorn sheep and a mama bear with her little cub were among the spectacular sights we enjoyed in the park. Our tour guide warned us if Mama Bear sensed we were there, she would be upon us in no time. We found it so hard to imagine this bear, with her fat rolly polly form, was able to move so swiftly.

One of my dreams had always been to go whitewater rafting on the Colorado River. Instead, we would be navigating down the Susitna River out of Talkeetna, south of Denali National Park. I couldn't wait!

Preparing for the trip, we donned slicker pants, jackets, hats and life jackets. Piling into the raft, the trip leaders instructed us to paddle especially hard when a whirlpool came into view because you could simply disappear into one of those powerful, whirling pits.

Each raft needed a bailer. Jack volunteered to be the

White-water rafting down the Susitna River in Alaska.

Jack and I by a magnificent glacier in Glacier Bay.

bailer for our raft. He had to bail so furiously the whole trip. The water moved so swiftly it could have easily inundated our raft. At the end of the trip, my desire for future whitewater rafting trips was more than satisfied. It was a wild and scary, yet exhilarating, experience.

In Kotzebue, a small Native Alaskan village located on the Bering Sea, we could sadly see the modern-day plight of these people. Most of them were inebriated, their boats strewn along the beach in all forms of decay. Our hearts went out to these people, but we both felt their dire circumstances resulted from a toxic mix of modernization and government over-subsidization.

Meeting Susan Butcher, four-time Iditarod sled dog race champion, proved a highlight of our trip while in Nome, Alaska. Susan lived there all summer, preparing her sled dog team for that unique and now world-famous race. She taught us to "mush" her team. Susan fed her dogs with salmon she had caught in rivers and streams herself. The puppies rolled around and captured my heart! Oh, how I wished I could've brought one home with me!

The sled dogs were not the only ones feasting on salmon, however. We ate copious amounts of mouthwatering salmon at the many open air "fish bakes" for which Alaska has become famous.

Cruising both arms of Glacier Bay, we gazed upon huge waves rising up as glaciers calved, releasing gushing rivers of water from their frozen glacial prisons.

I couldn't wait to see the puffin birds I had long read about. Large colonies of the colorful puffins swooped down from the outcroppings on the high cliffs. Wow – watching them plunge down from their nests high above entranced us for a good stretch of time!

Seals cavorted gracefully through the water around the ice floes around our boat. They seemed carefree as they bobbed, barked and slid all over! And then, glancing upwards, we spied a bald eagle gracefully gliding on the wind.

As we flew over majestic Mt. McKinley, now called Denali on our way home, the persistent cloud covering parted momentarily. Denali's dramatic beauty of jagged, snow-covered peaks took our breath away. The 5,500 mile journey we made, flying over the magnificent expanse of the 50th state, enraptured us, gifting us with memories to last a lifetime.

To this day, I am thrilled Alaska was at the top of Jack's bucket list.

A Visit to the Holy Land

One day, Jack emerged from his home office sporting a huge grin on his face.

"You must have a fun filled secret. What are you up to?" I teased him.

"Surprise, my Love! We will celebrate our tenth anniversary walking in the footsteps of Jesus! I know Israel is on the top of *your* bucket list," he exclaimed, a gleam in his eyes. "I'm taking you there to celebrate!"

Landing in Tel Aviv, we met our tour bus and one hour later arrived in Jerusalem. As soon as we settled into our hotel room, I announced to Jack, "I'm going to try to call Kevin!"

My heart skipped a beat as I heard Kevin's voice through the receiver, its rich English accent returning my greeting. It had been a full 11 years since Kevin had stayed with us. So much had changed. Gloriously, we would now reunite with our Jewish South African AFS exchange student, Kevin.

Those days when he interned at Barnes Hospital in St. Louis and had lived in our home seemed at once so long ago and yet just like yesterday. Now Dr. Kevin Tatz, he was living in Jerusalem with his wife, Suzanne, and their five children. Meeting Suzanne brought back special memories for Jack and me. We had the privilege of counseling Kevin on his marriage choice of Suzanne long ago. Little did she know, we actually played cupid in her life.

We were visiting Israel at the time of the Jewish fall celebration of *Sukkot*, the "Festival of the Booths." The man of the household builds a booth outside his house where he spends the week in religious study, prayers and devotions. The orthodox Jewish faith is principally a man's religion. Kevin invited Jack, a born-again Christian, to join him in the booth. It was a spiritual high for Jack to share with Kevin how the New Testament fulfilled the Old Testament celebrations and prophecies.

Kevin and I, reunited in Israel many years after his AFS exchange year.

While Jack was in the booth with Kevin, I enjoyed precious time with Suzanne and my lively Israeli surrogate grandchildren. We squeezed every spare moment we could together. We found, in our relationship with Kevin and Suzanne, a deep bond of mutual respect, a bridge of love across faith traditions.

Walking along the *Via Dolorosa* (also known as the twelve stages of the cross), the processional route in the Old City of Jerusalem where Jesus is believed to have walked on the way to his crucifixion, proved a profoundly emotional experience for us both. As I walked, I took great joy in tucking the prayers from my Community Bible Study class into the Wailing Wall. When we visited the Holocaust Museum, my heart felt heavy with grief. We felt as if, in the span of a week, we had soared to the mountain top, reuniting with Kevin, and plunged into the depths, the valley of the Holocaust.

The high chalk-colored cliffs we passed on the way to the Dead Sea contained the very scrolls of God's Law – the Ten Commandments – discovered by a shepherd boy, much like the one in the ancient world who rose to become "a man after God's own heart." Back in Jerusalem we viewed parts of sacred Scriptures in the Dead Sea Scroll museum. Visiting Jericho, Bethlehem, Masada and traveling through the Wadi made us feel as if we were living right in the pages of the Holy Bible. It was a joy how our faith came alive, verified true through sites, traditions, geography, architecture and artifacts for all the world to see.

Exploring Europe

Returning home, Jack found the latest edition of his hunting magazine in the mail.

One article leapt right off the page at him. "Discover Colonel Samuels' First-Class Couples' European Hunting Trips."

True to Jack's attention to detail and thorough nature, he contacted the Colonel, asking for references. The glowing recommendations included statements like, "This is a trip of a lifetime. Go even if you have to hock the family jewels!"

Each of Colonel Samuels' trips were limited to ten couples. Each day, the Colonel's wife, Lydia, conducted a tour for the accompanying wives while the husbands experienced traditional European hunting. Colonel Samuels always set aside one of the hunting days for the wives to accompany their husbands.

Our first trip with the Colonel was to Ireland and Wales. Aromatic, piping-hot Irish coffee greeted us upon arrival at the hunting lodge just outside of Dublin, such a gift on that cold blustery day.

At the crack of dawn the next morning, the eager hunters were off for their first day. We gals slept in and met up at 8:00am for a sumptuous breakfast together. Our private bus and private guide awaited us.

Soon we were off exploring the wonders of the

Emerald Isle! Esther, one of my newfound friends, told me on the day we were in Dublin she planned to go to Trinity College to view the Book of Kells. I ached to go with her to see the stunningly beautiful manuscript of the four gospels written by St. Jerome. Alas, I had committed to buying a set of Waterford crystal for a friend back home. Unfortunately for me, there wasn't time to do both.

Traveling by ferry from Ireland, we soon arrived in Wales. Our bus whisked us off for a scenic tour on our way to our lodging in a quaint Welsh village. The rugged rocks and rolling vistas, draped in lush greenery, mesmerized us.

Excitement reigned on our first night there. The staff at the inn, along with Colonel Samuels and all the locals, were breathless with anticipation. For this was *the day* when, all over the Welsh countryside, runners, dressed in traditional garb, would transport the first press of the season's wine to their fellow countrymen and women. The electrifying atmosphere surrounding this fall Welsh cultural affair drew us in.

Hunting day in Wales for the wives started off with a ride on a narrow-gauged, old, yellow-cog train. We rattled, bumped, and rolled along, descending into a deep, but broad, valley. There stood the hunting crew, ready for our arrival. We walked with our husbands, and the assigned field guide, to the reserved shooting location.

As we stood directly behind our husbands, the beaters – hunting professionals who rouse or drive game from cover – would "flush" the birds, scattering them far and wide. Our husbands took aim and fired, prompting the

Jack and I relaxing together with other couples on our first hunting trip with the Colonel.

field guide to retrieve any fallen birds.

Then tables appeared, spread with exquisite linen, china and cutlery, also filled up with overflowing glasses of the country's finest whiskey. The emcee offered a toast and a prayer of thanksgiving for the birds and anticipated meal. Our group felt enveloped in the arms of a culture and people proudly distinct in language and traditions from their more conspicuous neighbor, England.

Soon we were London-bound as we bid the charm of Wales and its people goodbye. Checking in to the Hyde Park Hotel, our room overlooked London's famous Harrods Department Store. We enjoyed exploring Harrod's vast food selection and exquisite fashions. Orators on designated daises in nearby Hyde Park, freely expressing their opinions on a wide range of subjects, captured our attention as well.

Flying home on the Irish carrier, Aer Lingus, Jack and I agreed – this trip *was* worth "hocking the family jewels!"

I commented to Jack, "You know, Colonel Samuels appears way past middle age. Even though it's likely to tax our budget, I think we should take all the trips of his we can!"

Jack agreed. And soon we were off again.

This time, we explored Scotland. Its lime and clay-mortared masonry buildings seemed to cast a greyish hue far and wide. The heather-covered moors greeted us as we headed to our destination on the North Sea. We arrived the second week of the annual European grouse hunt. Our hunting lodge was Prince Philip's abode for the first week of the hunting season. The Colonel's protocol was much the same as our trip in Ireland and Wales.

The Scottish hunting day for the wives was nothing like the sunny, calm day we had enjoyed in Wales. This time proved challenging, scary, and nearly tragic. We were dressed in rain gear and our "wellies." The Colonel instructed us to buy them for our shooting day. I thought to myself that should have been a clue of what lay ahead. One of those famous North Sea storms roared in just as we disembarked our bus for the shoot. We quickly found refuge in a large barn close by. Sitting on bales of hay, we consumed our box lunches.

As the first wave of the storm dissipated, we emerged to find an angry rushing creek in front of us. It was a dry bed when we arrived. This meant we had to ford the creek. We had to keep our balance while precariously traversing a log to get across.

One of the hunters accidentally slipped, crashing into the gushing stream! We reached down and grabbed him to keep him from drowning. We watched in disbelief at how swiftly his expensive gun got swept away. The wind started howling as we made our way uphill through the tangled heather ground cover. The force of the driving rain stung our eyes. I wondered if we were going to drown in our hunting blind, a deep concealing enclosure from which we could shoot grouse.

In spite of the weather, the beaters were still out, flushing the birds. When the rain slackened enough for Jack to see the birds, he would shoot. At the end of the day, Jack felt a sense of accomplishment. In spite of the elements of nature, he had shot grouse in Scotland!

I was just thankful it was over and we were safe. I climbed into a hot, steaming bath upon our return to the inn. *Ahh, what a soothing, luxurious safe haven!* The gourmet dinner and evening entertainment led into a much welcomed night of rest. In all our trips with Colonel Samuels, this was the only near-tragic event.

We spent our last day in Scotland enjoying castle life. After touring Edinburgh, we cruised a bit through Scotland's rugged countryside. Then a castle emerged from the rugged terrain. Going inside, we entered a cavernous room with a roaring fire and enjoyed some refreshments, followed by a sumptuous farewell dinner. The evening ended with Scottish entertainment, complete with traditional songs and dances.

The next morning we boarded our bus headed for the Edinburgh airport. We bid farewell to our new friends flying home, and picked up our rental car.

For us, driving on the left side of the road proved rather harrowing. We made it safely to St. Andrews, however, and checked into our hotel. Then we went to see if our names had been drawn from the golf lottery. We both yearned to play "The Old Course." The kind lady in the pro shop told us to return early in the morning.

Some of the wonderful Scottish entertainment we enjoyed on our trip with the Colonel.

Up extra early the next morning, we checked in at the pro shop. Our hearts leapt; we would get to play golf on the world-famous St. Andrews golf course that very day!

We'll forever be indebted to our helpful and patient caddy that day. For the heather rough would gobble up dozens of our errant golf balls. The large six-foot-deep sand traps were very deadly and intimidating. The privilege of playing on those hallowed grounds plus the opportunity to be in the very place where the game of golf began became a once-in-a-lifetime experience for us.

As we turned our rental car in at the Edinburgh airport, I turned to Jack and announced, "Surprise, my Love! I'm taking you on to Paris to celebrate your birthday!" Jack responded with a big grin.

The Louvre, the D'Orsay, and a tour of the Loire Valley proved the icing on the cake for our Scotland adventure. As we headed home, we savored the moments from this yet-again extraordinary trip with the Colonel, topped off with our extra jaunt to gay Paris!

Not long after returning home, yet another communiqué from the Colonel arrived inviting us to join his Portugal hunt. Even though Jack was suffering severe back pain at the time, he was still eager to go. Wheeling Jack through the airport to board our flight, I thought to myself,

How ludicrous is this! Pushing a man in a wheelchair to catch a flight to Portugal to go hunting. Because the shoot would be in strict European style, it became possible for Jack to go.

Flying into Lisbon, Portugal, we soon settled into Posada de Pomelo, our hotel. We spent the evening with our future ranch host, Bico, and his charming wife, Catarina. This delightful young couple was the sixth generation in the family-owned business, a sprawling ranch called Vale Do Manantio.

The Portuguese countryside, lush with olive groves, captivated us. Cork trees lined many of the roadways. Along the way we saw a number of small donkey-drawn wagons, pitched high with hay. Perched on high hills stood crumbling castles. The red-tiled roof adobe villages looked old and tired. It seemed very much like an underdeveloped country.

On our way to LaDoeiro, Portugal for a four day shoot, we stopped at the Ramalho's cattle ranch. Caballeros in full dress welcomed us, offering us their horses to ride. During our conversations, we met one caballero who came yearly to the Salinas rodeo, nearby to our home in the States. I thought to myself, *How exceptionally rare to meet a rodeo rider in the vast plains of Portugal so familiar with our part of the world!* Indeed, I felt like he was the world traveler, not me.

Ramalho's ranch bred and raised bulls for the bull fights. In their corral they demonstrated the basics of bullfighting. They called out, "Any volunteers?" One of our brave crew took the challenge. This is just one example of the many unique events the Colonel included in his hunting trips.

Arriving at Bico's and Catarina's ranch, Vale Do Manantio, the staff lined up to welcome us. We got our room assignments along with a Madeira aperitif, a specialty the Portuguese are famous for. Aware we were celebrating our anniversary, Colonel Samuels had ordered a large suite for us. Our oversized bathroom sported stunning blue and white tile in a floral motif. From the large bedroom window, we could gaze out on a large herd of sheep grazing on the ranch terrain.

At our gourmet dinner in the evening we learned how fortunate we were. Our fellow travelers found their accommodations less than luxurious.

The wives' hunt the following day on the casual side and ended with a cookout close to the high hill where the shoot had been held. This experience was a far cry from the other formal European hunts, yet it proved memorably delightful.

Flying home, Jack and I reflected on this hunt. Of all our hunting trip with the Colonel so far, Portugal stood out as the most primitive. At the same time, the country's history, dating back to Roman times, seemed to permeate and enhance the country's ambiance.

Just when we thought we would settle back into

"normal life" back home, we found ourselves holding another letter addressed from the Colonel. This time, he invited us on a trip to the Czech Republic.

Intrigued, we fantasized about it for a bit, but then came back to reality. This time, we felt as if we simply could not afford the time or financial commitment.

Some days later, the phone rang and it was Colonel Samuels. He called to strongly urge us to reconsider. It sounded like an outstanding trip, but we had already made our decision not to go. One week later he called again saying, "I really want you two to go on this trip. I'll give you the trip for half price."

Shocked, Jack and I thanked him profusely and told him we'd attempt to make some schedule changes and join the tour.

Four weeks later we were en route to Prague.

Getting settled on our flight, I hung my small purse on the arm of my seat next to the window. Jack always requested a window seat for me on our flights. He knew how much I enjoyed the sights that prompted my inner voice to say, "Nearer my God to Thee." And, being an avid photographer, I often took pictures out of the plane's window. I made a mental note to not forget my purse.

Landing in Vienna for the last leg of our flight into Prague, we stepped through the large airport doors. Instantly in a panic, I exclaimed, "Jack, my purse with my passport is still on the plane!"

We whirled around to take one step outside, thinking we could run back to our plane parked on the tarmac nearby.

But the doors were already locked. Telling the guard at the door our dilemma, he said, "Go up the escalator, turn left, go down the hall and tell your problem to the person there."

At the same time, Colonel Samuels called out to us, "We're boarding. You will have to catch the next flight out." We jumped on the escalator, running with it, turned left at the top, ran down the hall to a desk and breathlessly explained our predicament.

With great calmness and efficiency,, the gentleman made a phone call.

Turning to us he said, "Mrs. Wulfmeyer, your purse will be delivered to the checkout desk."

Thanking him profusely, we ran down the escalator to the desk. The attendant smiled and checked my passport. Handing me my purse she told us, "A cart and driver are outside the door waiting for you." The driver zoomed us to our plane. Breathlessly, we uttered a thank you and hastened up the stairs just as the flight crew was closing the doors. We had made it!

As we boarded, everyone on our tour cheered. With my heart beating furiously, but my heart full of gratitude, my reddened countenance slowly faded. The tight security and efficiency, as well as the Viennese sensitivity to our situation, so impressed us.

Our panic-stricken start to our Czech Republic trip was only that. Everything else proved smooth and delightful. As we stepped into the Prague Palace Hotel's private dining room for our arrival dinner, an elegantly-set table of sparkling foot-high crystal wine glasses and fine china greeted us.

With a formal welcome from the Colonel, we all soon were enjoying the fine wine and food. That evening set the stage for our entire tour.

While in Prague, we took in its world-famous sights. The picturesque old town of St. Vitus Church with its castle, framed in fall colors, captivated me. Wenceslas Square, sporting its world-famous Astronomical Clock and iconic downtown area, was within walking distance of our hotel. The Colonel had reserved a private street car for our tour of the city. He hired an accordian player to play Czech music as we viewed the twelve bridges over the Charles River and its environs. Strolling through the Jewish quarter, some craftsmen invited us into their glass shop. There, they demonstrated their fine glass-blowing techniques. They generously offered a chance to any of us who wished to try it out. Our hunting friend, Leroy, jumped at the opportunity.

Saying goodbye to captivating Prague, we were on our way to Častolovice castle. The Colonel had two events planned along the way. Our bus suddenly pulled off the road. Alighting onto the fresh emerald turf, we fabulously received our introduction to the art of falconry.

In a moment dripping with tense anticipation, we gazed at these exquisite birds perched on their handler's shielded leathered arms. They then launched the falcons off into the air. Well trained, the birds quickly returned to perch on the familiar arm of their handler. We could view their magnificent markings and powerful talons up close. Jack and I felt so grateful to experience one of God's creations so intimately.

As lunchtime arrived, our bus driver suddenly turned into a dense forest. Disembarking, we followed a path leading to an open air shelter sporting tables and benches. Chefs greeted us and immediately served up huge bowls of steaming soup.

We seemed to devour the mouthwatering vegetable beef soup, along with grilled sausages and other items, in an instant. The group was, yes, that hungry.

As we finished, two handsome pairs of horses, each set pulling a wagon, arrived. Clambering upon the wagon benches, we took an extended ride through a thick forest dotted with oak trees and sprinkled with golden aspens. Among the trees, we could see white deer with massive racks and ferocious Russian wild black boar.

As we emerged from the dense forest, a tranquil lake greeted us, complete with snow white swans floating serenely across the water and horses and donkeys grazing in the distance.

When we arrived at the town and castle of Častolovice, Diane Sternberg Ova Phipps, the owner of the castle, greeted us. At our luxurious dinner that evening, she briefly shared how she was able to return to her family's 12th-century castle in 1992. Following the Czechoslovakian "Velvet Revolution" and the departure of the Soviets, the miracle of restitution started. People who qualified could reclaim their family's property, and this included the castle. Diane qualified for the return of Častolovice.

Diane frequently joined the women in our group as

we lingered over breakfast. She told us many fascinating personal stories. Diane even had written a book of the castle's history, sharing about the life she led escaping the Communists at eight years old. I was thrilled to purchase her autobiography entitled *The Journey* in the castle gift shop. Diane wrote a personal note and autographed it for me. I treasure this personal glimpse into the vanishing world of European aristocracy.

Častolovice stood in the center of expansive grounds and surrounding forest, allowing for extended walks on the property and in the woods. White deer roamed freely; our presence did not seem to disturb them at all! The cattle and emus rested in a barn nearby. I delighted in photographing these creatures in their quiet, pastoral environment.

We were treated to a 17th-century-style formal hunting banquet in the castle, precluded by a reception in the great hall. At one end stood a lovely intimate chapel. Diane told us this was the very location where she was christened. She escorted us to the dining room. There, before our eyes, a display of wild game with all the trimmings appeared, seemingly straight out of a Van Dyke painting. An evening of dancing to the accompaniment of a musical ensemble followed.

Vienna was the icing on the cake for this phenomenal trip. Our hotel stood immediately across the street from the Schönbrunn Palace. Our private farewell dinner took place in the palace. Before the food was served, we could take a personal tour of the grand palace rooms. A four-piece Viennese string quartet greeted us as we entered the dining room, filling our mealtime with delicious sounds from this most famous epicenter of classical music.

Boarding the planes for our flights home, Colonel Samuels told us this was his last hunting trip. Now 80, he was beginning to have difficulty walking. He surely went out in a blaze of glory with this trip. We thanked him profusely for the favor he showed us, and for the four fantastic hunting trips we had enjoyed with him. Those trips were certainly worth "hocking the family jewels for." And more.

10

Lifesaving Creations

Jonquil
Fragrance of Love

One day in the late 1980's, Jack burst into the room, a huge grin on his face, announcing, "Susie, I've found our home!"

We had been living in the gated community in Walnut Creek, but had felt that was a temporary holding ground for something better. We had sighted out some communities in the area and were excited about prospects in Danville, a lovely community just 10 miles south.

"Buy it," I responded without hesitation to Jack.

Later, when I told Holly, she immediately scolded me.

"Mom, you can't let Jack buy a house you haven't even seen!"

"Actually, Holly, I can. I know it's the right one because it meets everything on the list of 12 qualities we wanted in a new home. And, I trust Jack's judgment implicitly."

With this new home, another desire of my heart was fulfilled: having a swimming pool in my backyard. One of my favorite activities had been swimming. But way back in 1956, when Howard built our home in St. Louis, we had three acres of rolling lawn. It was beautiful, but a swimming pool at that time was out of the question. Still, that is when I discovered the joy of gardening, another desire of the heart.

Psalm 37:4 tells us to "Delight [ourselves] in the Lord, and he will give [us] the desires of [our] heart[s]." I've always been impressed how our first desire must be in God, and out of that He unfolds these desires in His perfect timing.

Dreams do come true. Mine were more than fulfilled with our move to Danville. Not only did our new home have a large, kidney-shaped pool, complete with diving board, water slide and connecting spa, the property also had a skillfully landscaped garden. Once again, my restoring God had given me a garden, even adding a fruit orchard producing fresh delights for us to enjoy.

One particular day while I was out enjoying our new yard, I couldn't help but overflow with thankfulness for this gift of a garden *and* an orchard. As the aromas of the lemons and roses transported me, I began to notice apples almost ready to be picked. I thought to myself, "I'll make a fresh apple pie." I could almost taste it warm out of the oven, topped with a scoop of vanilla ice cream!

So much of our home in Danville felt right. We got along well with several of our neighbors. They often took care of our cats, yard and mail as we enjoyed a new season of travel, not for business, but now for pleasure, and mostly overseas. Because of these faithful neighbors, we left home with a sense of security we'd return to the same place we had left. And when we did, our home seemed to embrace us, warmly welcoming us into its arms of love and comfort.

Unfortunately, all this would come to an end much earlier than we had wished. For upon returning to those golden hills and our dream home in Danville after our trip to Israel, I was forced to face a growing physical problem. While we still lived in Walnut Creek, I had started to experience strange physical symptoms.

The first episode happened as I was playing golf. I became very fatigued to the point of whiffing the ball. Then tears rolled down my cheeks. Jack and I were both mystified by my utter lack of precision mingled with exhaustion.

Not long after, stomach cramps, shortness of breath and headaches began to accompany my fatigue.

One evening, our phone rang. It was Sarah, from my Bible Study Fellowship group.

"Sue, turn on your television to Channel 6. They're running a feature on a health problem that sounds a lot like yours, the one we've been praying about."

In the feature, two pilots who had been flying on patrol suddenly awakened to discover they had been unconscious for over an hour. Later, they learned a Chevron refinery had expelled a huge phenol cloud the day they happened to be flying over the area.

Their frightening experience happened at the same time I had my first golf incident. Jack and I stared at each other wondering if that might be what had affected me. We knew the prevailing winds blew toward us from Pittsburg, California, the location of several refineries.

We began to observe I felt much better on our trips out of the area. We also started to note the fumes from jets when we traveled by air began affecting me more and more. We had hoped our move from Walnut Creek to Danville (further from Pittsburg) would help. Instead, my health issues intensified exponentially. My nighttime sleep was intermittent. I could only sleep an hour at a time. My heart often went into arrythmia.

We consulted doctors.They ran many tests which all showed I was perfectly healthy. My craving for meat was constant. That was scary. All the latest health articles had grave warnings about consuming too much meat.

One bright sunny day we heard a knock at the door. There was our new neighbor, Janice. She had a copy of her latest *Reader's Digest*.

"Sue, you must read this article." She pointed to the title. I stood, almost in shock.

My House is Killing Me, it read.

Thanking Janice profusely, we pored over it.

Stunned, I wondered, "Could this be me?"

Jack researched every possible aspect of our house or our yard. He had multiple tests run. I took the article to the fourth doctor I was seeing. "Doctor, could this be me?"

Reading the article, he responded, "Sue, we didn't have any allergy training in medical school. I recommend you see an allergist. There is one who is world-renowned in nearby Berkeley."

After a one-half-hour consultation, the allergist turned to me and spoke. "You are chemically allergic. There is no allergy test to prove your condition. I know because I am also chemically allergic. We will take you through the battery of allergy tests to see if you have other allergies." The results showed I was allergic to chicken, eggs, and turkey.

I became a voracious reader on the topic of allergies. I learned allergic reactions rob one of protein. Little wonder why I craved meat so much. Thankfully, I hadn't followed the health articles. I had said to Jack, "If those articles are all true, I will die from eating meat."

In 1991, on doctor's orders due to my life-threatening chemical allergic reactions, we had to move. My doctor had said, "Sue, you need to make a choice of living either in the mountains or near the ocean. It's there you will find the purest air available so you can continue living. Which do you choose?"

My immediate response was, "The ocean."

Jack knew the ocean's pure air meant Carmel to me. We had visited that quaint, artsy community located on the California central coast numerous times and had fallen in love with it. Jack immediately found a place to rent right across from the ocean. I walked the entire length of Carmel beach twice a day. Each weekend, Jack came to see me. He grew more and more excited. My health was showing signs of improving. He immediately put our Danville dream home on the market priced to sell. One month later, we sold our Danville home at 9am and bought our Carmel home at 11am the same day! Thinking my travel adventures had ceased, I was very thankful I could live out my life in one of the most beautiful places on earth.

A quote from William E. Stafford's poem, "The Well Rising," expresses our hearts for God's creation: "I plant my feet with care in such a world." The roar of crashing waves greet us each morning in our new Carmel home. We can see mighty waves crashing upon the rocky shores of Point Lobos in the distance from our master bedroom.

The magnificent Pacific Ocean – just six short blocks from our new home – means the pure salt air continually fills my lungs, even to this day. Salt, with its healing properties, gradually caused my chemical allergies to decline.

On a quiet morning, we can hear birdsong mixed with the siren-like serenade of sea lions. All this reminds us of the steadfastness and the harmony of our world, for surely this has been going on for thousands of years. The vast expanse of the beach brings to our minds how God's love for us is greater than all the grains of sand on all the beaches of the world.

Brilliant warblers, finches and golden-crowned song sparrows would often awaken us with their perfectly tuned symphony. Perhaps this is the way they express their gratitude for their free breakfast! Bird feeders nestled into our picturesque California Live Oak trees have consistently been part of our garden since we arrived.

We turn our gaze to our garden from our second story bedroom window. The vibrant, unfolding flower blossoms burst with every color on an artist's palette. We feel as if we are surrounded with riches of pure gold. These abundant, free treasures cause our hearts to yearn to love, to cherish, to enrich and to give back.

Teamwork abounds in our Carmel garden. Jack, my

engineer, orchestrates the drip irrigation system. He checks and rechecks to be certain each plant gets just the right amount of water. He uses weed killer with great caution. He tweaked his engineering know-how to light up the magnificent live oak trees against the night sky. I design, dig, and plant.

Order abounds in our garden. The mighty oaks forever dispatch their leaves down to mulch the garden. They keep our plants moist and free of pesky weeds. Earthworms labor, continually transforming our compost into rich decomposed soil. Blue jays, titmice, and chickadees devour with delight the insects intent on destruction. Brilliant iridescent red and green hummingbirds, shod with pollen, flit from flower to flower, enhancing their beauty as they carry out their duty to cross-pollinate.

BB and CC, our beloved kittens, commonly known as tuxedo cats, work prodigiously to eliminate the gophers and voles intent on devouring plants appealing to their palate. We applaud our kittens' efforts with great praise. At the same time, we discourage their exuberance when it comes to catching alligator lizards and snakes for play. Even though they are a vital part of our horticulture team, BB and CC just don't seem to understand these creatures, too, are God's creations.

Our garden, on the corner of Fourteenth and Fifteenth Avenues, welcomes many visitors. They come from all over the world. Some come for a short visit, staying at Clint Eastwood's world-renowned Mission Ranch just across the

BB (left) and CC (right) relaxing by our picture window.

street. Others hail from parts all over the U.S.; they come to discover and enjoy the ambiance of charming Carmel. They catch me lovingly caring for our garden, and they frequently stop to admire it. Often, I am able to share the love of Christ with them and pass along a Jesus DVD as we connect more deeply.

Energetic young children often skip happily by our garden on their way to Carmel River School across the street. Kindergarteners through fifth graders often call out as they pass, "We love your garden!" Sometimes we share our garden with them, allowing them to choose a flower or two as a gift for their teachers.

Carmelites are known for adoring their canine friends. Walking by with their dogs, they pause to enjoy the profusion of color and aroma. Being an animal lover myself, I so enjoy stopping my gardening to chat and offer my affection to these new furry friends. Our garden gives generously of its many plants and trees and love to all who express interest.

When our grandsons Spencer and Parker were little ones, they would sometimes come to visit Grandpa and Nana. Then the garden became a jungle in deepest Africa! Stalking lions and tigers lurk in the enormous, deep green acanthus leaves; tall blades of lilies of the Nile prompt their spirit of daring adventure.

The boys climb the sprawling branches of the oak trees like energetic monkeys. Spencer, in particular, finds those large meandering branches an ideal place to relax. He spends chunks of time zoning into his own world there.

I love spending time tending to our beautiful garden by our home in Carmel, California.

He's always been a contemplative type.

Forget-me-nots, daisies and a multitude of other flora offer perfect locations for hiding Easter eggs. With their competitive spirits, on the signal "go," the entire family attempts to find every egg in our garden. We have great fun together at our annual family gathering to celebrate Resurrection Day. Often days, weeks and months pass, and I'll discover an unfound hidden egg; it always brings a smile to my heart.

We place our feet with care in God's creation to leave a rich heritage for generations to come. The footprints in our garden echo around the world the treasure of this free gift. The footprints of our grandsons, cast in stepping stones each year when they were young, announce with joy their yearly growth.

Entertaining gives Jack and me an opportunity to share our gift of hospitality. We thrive on loving people.

A wide, curving brick walk leads through the garden to the welcome mat placed on the doorstep of our two-story gray and white colonial home. As guests enter through our front door, our interior design of vintage furnishings greets them. Most often, this evokes exclamations of "Oh, what a warm, comfortable, and cozy home!" In fact, our home has been dubbed the "Leave It To Beaver" home after the 1950's family sitcom.

As people enter our home, their eyes often immediately alight on the living room's focal point: a tall curved glass étagère displaying antique art glass. Artists from around the world created these unique pieces in the late 1800s. Encased on one of the glass shelves sit two elegant satin glass rose bowls. These bowls inspired my mother and stepfather, Carrie and Martin Love, to study and collect these exquisite works of art.

These two particular rose bowls have their own story to tell you. They sat atop a massive mahogany article of furniture in my grandparents' spacious farmhouse. These two delicate satin rose bowls are the only fragile survivors of the tragic fire that totally destroyed their former home in the fall of 1930. But instead of being thankful for being saved and appreciated, it seems they were continually arguing and complaining.

The ombre pink-toned bowl usually started off with a taunt: "Look at me, I'm much more elegant and softer than you are." Then the ombre yellow bowl would retort, "Anyone who looks at me knows *I'm* the most exquisite, with my white opalescent base gradually shading to a striking yellow at my neck."

Then they'd begin to express their discontent with the people they lived with. Peering down at the four-year-old girl living with them, that being me at the time, they would comment in disgust, "Look at that bratty girl! She never even notices us. She doesn't care a fig for us. All she wants to do is play outside all the time and pay attention to those stinky farm animals. Even our owner fails to see how we are now all covered with dust!"

The only positive opinion they had was about my Mother, Carrie Elizabeth Jorgenson Gray Love. They noticed her loving, covetous eyes cast their way when she was around. The pink-toned bowl declared, "Someday, I want to belong to her!"

"Dream on you silly thing, what makes you think *that* would ever happen?" retorted the yellow bowl.

"Well, dreams do come true, you know," replied the pink bowl.

Fast-forward 20 years and that dream did, indeed, come true. That "bratty" four-year-old was now a college graduate, married with a growing family. Their original owners, my grandparents, had died, and now the bowls were happily sitting together in Carrie's living room, elegantly displayed. Her loving, meticulous care transformed them. They gained self worth and became illuminating objects of art as they learned real beauty springs from inner peace. It fills one with contentment. And even though a multitude of newer exquisite glass objects surrounded them, they basked in knowing *they* were the inspiration for the magnificent collection.

Then major tragedy struck. The one who loved and cared for them died. Their world suddenly fell apart and all was chaos.

"Oh, what is going to happen to us?" they wailed. "Who will love and appreciate us? Oh, no, not that bratty four-year-old, now a mother with boisterous grade school children! Oh, woe is us! She never cared a fig for us. We'll just sit in her house praying we don't get broken and collecting dust. No one will pay any attention to us. We will just be worthless objects!"

There they sat bickering again about which one was the most beautiful and complaining about the family they were with. They didn't even notice the large glass case the master of the household meticulously designed and built for the cherished collection they now were part of.

One day when they were in ugly spirits, feeling sorry for themselves, strange events transpired. Boxes appeared along with wrapping paper and funny clear stuff covered with bubbles. To their consternation, that bratty four-year-old of the past carefully took each one, wrapping each in many layers of bubbles, and placed it in the box. Then she closed the lid. What followed was absolutely terrifying. Little did they know as they bounced and bumped along, they were part of a shipment making its way from St. Louis, Missouri to Walnut Creek, California.

Yes, they knew life would be horrible with that bratty four-year-old. This same excruciating experience happened two more times as they moved first to Danville, and then to Carmel. Thankfully, the second and third trips proved more manageable. Still, life seemed to have so many twists and turns, so much darkness and separation. Things seemed even worse than they could have ever imagined!

It was then they experienced a second miracle. To their amazement, that bratty four-year-old, now a grandmother, carefully and lovingly unwrapped each of them. She lovingly placed them in a mirrored-glass display case.

Both rose bowls became the center of attention, even as they became surrounded by other antique glass treasures. Admirers oohed and awed over them as their new owner removed each one to be caressed and stroked. Her friends, touching their cool, smooth satin finish and admiring their brilliant shadings of pink and yellow, would take in their beauty.

Before long, they became perfectly content sitting side-by-side, loving their new life and each other. They had learned the true meaning of the perfect gift: when one is filled with overflowing divine love, one is filled with love for others. Love erases jealousy, quarreling, feelings of rejection and falling into harsh judgment of others. This former bratty four-year-old knows personally that in different ways they really had been loved for seventy-six years and will continue to be loved by her children.

When visitors come for an extended visit, a collection of teddy bears offer them greetings and hugs. These teddys line the wall of our guest bedroom. Most are ones I've received as gifts from family and friends along this journey of life. But two of them I crafted with my own hands.

The bears have a story to tell you of their family, fortune and fame.

Many of these lovingly-made teddys have stories to tell...

...including my grandson Parker's teddy bear, pictured above.

In Ray Bradbury's book entitled *Zen in the Art of Writing,* he lists his seven writing tips. One tip, "Run Fast, Stand Still" leapt right off the page at me. That describes my teddy bears!

"Yeah," they shouted at me, "We've been your patient muses standing still all this time and now we want to run."

The two bears handcrafted by me want to tell you a larger story. It's the story of how, for more than 30 years, I've designed and created close to 100 bears, all but two which have found homes in a variety of places all over the globe.

One bear tells the story of how he became an integral part of my grandson Parker's life.

"My master, Parker Jones, is my creator's grandson. My great grandfather, an architect, exquisitely drafted my design. Then my great grandmother pieced me together. She shaped me into what I look like today."

"Look at us all, handcrafted by the mistress of this house. We're all dressed up in our special attire. We are baby gifts waiting for our tiny masters or mistresses to grow as big as we are, so they can wear our clothes. Our little boys will look like us. We are train engineers, cowboys, baseball and basketball players, and Mickey Mouse, and we will tag along with them while they play."

"We little girls get to go to birthday parties in our fancy dresses with matching shoes and bows in our hair. Look at me with my ultrasuede body, pink taffeta dress and mink boa, hat, and pompom- topped pink shoes. Oh, don't miss my dangling earrings and my gloves and purse! I'm personifying an elegant lady who once wore my furs to fancy parties in Washington D.C.!"

Seventy of these are known as "fur bears with charity spirits."

"We are irresistible with our soft, cuddly mink fur and sparkling glass eyes made in Germany. We go off to charity fundraisers with special tags listing Bible Scripture promises of God stuffed inside. Some of us have individually raised over sixteen hundred dollars for our favorite charity."

"In fact, seventy-five of the bears from our mistress' collection marched off to fight with U.S. soldiers in Iraq. Sergeant Mark Francis of the United States Marine Corp sent our mistress a letter entitled, *Teddy Bear Saves Soldiers*, telling of our heroism:

Beautiful,

Just wanted to write to you and tell you another story about an experience we had over here.

As you know, I asked for toys for the Iraqi children and several people (Americans that support us) sent them over by the box. On each patrol we take through the city, we take as many toys as will fit in our pockets and hand them out as we can. The kids take the toys and run to show them off as if they were worth a million bucks. We are as friendly as we can be to everyone we see, but especially so with the kids. Most of them don't have any idea what is going on and are completely innocent in all of this.

On one such patrol, our lead security vehicle stopped in the middle of the street. This is not normal and is very unsafe, so the following vehicles began to inquire over the radio. The lead vehicle reported a little girl sitting in the road and said she just would not budge. The command vehicle told the lead to simply go around her and to be kind as they did. The street was wide enough to allow this maneuver and so they waved to her as they drove around.

As the vehicles went around her, I soon saw her sitting there and in her arms she was clutching a little bear that we had handed her a few patrols back. Feeling an immediate connection to the girl, I radioed that we were going to stop. The rest of the convoy paused and I got out the make sure she was OK. The little girl looked scared and concerned, but there was a warmth in her eyes toward me. As I knelt down to talk to her, she moved over and pointed to a mine in the road. Immediately a cordon was set as the Marine convoy assumed a defensive posture around the site. The mine was destroyed in place.

It was the heart of an American that sent that toy. It was the heart of an American that gave that toy to that little girl. It was the heart of an American that protected that convoy from that mine. Sure, she was a little Iraqi girl, and she had no knowledge of purple mountain's majesty or fruited plains. It was a heart of acceptance, of tolerance, of peace and grace, even through the inconveniences of conflict that saved that convoy from hitting that mine. Those attributes are what keep Americans' hearts beating. She may have no affiliation at all with the United States, but she knows what it is to be brave. And if we can continue to support her and her new *government, she will know what it is to be free. Isn't that what Americans are, the free and the brave?*

If you sent over a toy for a Marine (US service member), you took part in this. You are a reason that Iraq has to believe in a better future. Thank you so much for supporting us and for supporting our cause over here .

Semper Fi, Mark J. Francis GySgt / USMC

"Well, of course, there are those of us who are just plain cloth or fake fur with a simple ribbon around our necks. We all have our own style for you. Inside us is our true nature, our heart. We yearn to run and leap into your arms to hug and love you unconditionally. To reassure you that no matter what your circumstances, you can squeeze us, hang on tight and know tomorrow will be better."

"How do we know this? Every one of us is stuffed with some of God's promises. They are a truth that never changes. Just look at a few from hundreds in God's Word, the Bible.

"I can do all things through Christ who strengthens me." Philippians 4:13

"With God all things are possible." Matthew 19:26

"I will instruct you and guide you along the best pathway for your life; I will advise you and watch your progress." Psalm 32:8

"The Lord is with you; his power gives you victory. The Lord will take delight in you, and in his love he will give you new life." Zephaniah 3:17

Here, I hold one of the many fur bears I have made over the years.

The bears wear a tag around their necks listing all the promises they are stuffed with.

"Our creator has dedicated each one of us to her mother," they declare proudly. "After all, because of her mother, she learned how to sew with love and persistent patience. Our creator's heart and hands fashioned us with scissors, sewing machine, needle and thread, snapped our joints together, stuffed us, and gave us our eyes, noses and lips."

They go on. "Now, collectively, we run fast and shout out loudly, 'We love you, world!' as we stand waiting for you to gather us in your arms, so we can hug each other for all eternity."

11

Splashing Puzzles

Gladiolus

Strength of Character and faithfulness

Jack and I had a heart for serving our community. As my health continued to improve, we began volunteering at the Sunset Center, Carmel's cultural venue. We were invited to become Monterey Symphony board members. We declined because we felt it might draw us away from our core commitment to Christian ministry.

On occasion, chatting with other Carmelites, we would share about our decision to decline serving on the Monterey Symphony board. They would react in utter shock when they heard. "You did what? No one turns down that prestigious position!" We would just smile, telling them we were happy being ushers. So happy we continued volunteering as ushers for the symphony and the world-famous Bach Festival for some 22 years!

Golf is a big deal in our part of the world, especially with the world-renowned Pebble Beach Golf Course attracting not only the annual AT&T Tournament, but also three U.S. Opens during the time we served as volunteers. We had so much fun serving in some of these major events. We were able to meet world-class golfers, and they inspired us to try to improve our game. We especially appreciated how the AT&T channelled much of their profits from these events to local community charities.

One of our assignments at the AT&T tournament was to care for the players and their families. It included taking messages for the players, sending their laundry off to the cleaners, making dinner reservations, and guarding the entrances to their hospitality tent. Those allowed in the tent were required to show proper credentials. This included the players as well. We had the distinction of meeting the world's top golfers and their families.

Many famous people entered our hallowed tent, but only if they had proper badges of identification.

We had two separate occasions handling the rich and famous we remember well. Jack was manning the entrance one day, and in walked our current President, Donald Trump, and his bodyguards. Jack politely inquired, "Sir, where are your entrance badges?"

Mr. Trump responded, "Don't you know who I am?"

"Most certainly, Mr. Trump," Jack responded. "But we have a strict protocol for everyone entering the players' private tent." Our leader, observing the situation, quickly took care of the matter. No surprise – I had a similar experience a few years prior with Rush Limbaugh.

We also served a number of years for the Concours d'Elegance extravaganza. Locals call this event "Car Week."

The Vintage Car Tour of the Monterey Peninsula happened on the Thursday of the event every year. We were tasked with registering the owners of these prestigious cars for the event. These owners came from around the world; the event had a true international flavor, making me feel as if I got to travel all over the planet simply by volunteering.

Jack became an active member of the Carmel Rotary Club. With his gift of organization, he launched a new professional directory for the club. Once completed, he also kept it current for ten years.

The annual Carmel Authors & Ideas Festival brought expert motivational authors and educators from around the world to our new cherished hometown. Most of the activity buzzed around the Sunset Center. Jack and I always got involved. Listening to the impressive array of gifted speakers proved a thrill. On the weekend of the festival, the authors and educators spoke to adults. But on the Thursday and Friday before, elementary, middle, and senior high school students were given the opportunity to experience this annual festival as well. My teacher's heart delighted in all this, for sure.

Jack and I, volunteering at the 2008 AT&T Pebble Beach National Pro-Am.

Jack and I, volunteering at the Concours d'Elegance "Car Week."

Carmel Presbyterian Church (CPC) was *the* church we visited our first Sunday in the area. We braved quite a crowd to attend. Sitting in the back row helped protect me from perfume and hair spray filling the sanctuary. There was too much danger of breathing deeply in a room full of people. We were continually on guard for chemicals I might inhale. Jack was my chemical detective with his excellent sense of smell. He warned me when his olfactory system kicked into gear, detecting anything harmful to me. The protective charcoal mask I wore was embarrassing; however, it did allow me to attend. But my delight in singing my favorite hymns had ceased for a time.

Walking into church that Sunday, we were in for a big surprise. Instantly, we recognized the pastor. Their interim pastor had been the same interim pastor in our former church, Danville Community Presbyterian Church! Upon seeing us, he immediately recognized and addressed Jack. "Jack," he implored, "I desperately need your help as my business manager." He knew of Jack's MBA in finance and excellent organizational skills.

Praying together that evening we cried out, "Lord, are you calling Jack to fill this role, even when we are just unpacking?" Not to mention, we were still running G&R Sales in the San Francisco Bay Area! God gave us the answer through our devotional Closer Walk one morning, using Romans 11:29, a verse explaining how God's gifts and his call are irrevocable. Jack certainly had the God-given gifts, and he felt called as well. The Word of God made the choice crystal clear. Jack became CPC's new volunteer business manager.

No sooner had we walked in our new front door, we heard the phone ringing. It was Sue, a former Community Bible Study group leader from the Bay Area. Having been on the Servants Team, I had trained her for Community Bible Study group leadership. Her family had moved to Carmel from the San Francisco East Bay a year earlier.

Her familiar voice brimmed with excitement. "Sue, we need to start Community Bible Study on the Monterey Peninsula!"

Here we were, brand-spanking new arrivals to Carmel. Sue's challenge simply overwhelmed me. My doctors last words still rang in my ears. "If you breathe enough of the healing salt air, you *may* live."

Following my doctor's orders, I walked from one end to the other of Carmel beach twice a day. I reveled in running my bare feet in the sand and surf. Watching the sea lions cavort so close to the shore, I felt like I could just scoop them up in my arms! The clean, cool ocean air refreshed my body and soul.

Over four months I prayed and walked the beach. *Was my Lord ready to take me home or would He heal me?* I pondered. And I prayed, "Lord is it possibly your plan to heal me? Am I to be used by you, Lord, to start a women's interdenominational Bible study on the Monterey Peninsula?" God kept using that same Scripture He had used for Jack, Romans 11:29, almost ceaselessly flooding my heart and mind.

I'll admit, it was with some fear and trepidation I responded, "Yes, Lord," to His call to serve. My thought was, *Well, if I accept this challenge and die serving You, Lord, what better thing could I possibly be doing when I see You face to face?*

Consulting the area director of Community Bible Study, the wheels were set in motion: GO! As one Christian friend put it, "You two hit the ground running!" Little did we know then, this was just the beginning.

An announcement caught our eyes one Sunday in the CPC bulletin. A new ministry opportunity had sprung up in our area: International Student's, Incorporated, or ISI. The bulletin called us to "Come and learn about ISI from Kert and Lillie Hultgren," two of CPC's members. Listening to their presentation, excitement swelled in both of our hearts. We looked at each other and exclaimed, "Wow, *what an opportunity* to connect with and help internationals!" Eagerly, we immediately signed up to host college and graduate-level international students from both the Monterey Institute of International Studies (MIIS, now called the Middlebury

Institute of International Studies at Monterey) and our local junior college, Monterey Peninsula College, or MPC.

Over the two-plus decades of our involvement, we enjoyed the privilege of befriending students from Japan, China, Korea, Siberia, Taiwan and Kenya, often hosting them for meals in our home. We enjoyed all these students so much, but two especially impacted our lives.

J.P. hailed from China. Sitting next to us at a large ISI event, J.P. turned to us and asked, "How does one actually become a Christian?"

We responded, "You accept Jesus Christ as your Lord and Savior." Filled with dozens of new students, the din in the jam-packed room made an in-depth conversation difficult. We recommended J.P. discuss his question with Kert Hultgren.

Answering our phone in the evening, it was J.P. sounding very excited. "Jack, Sue, I have prayed with Kert and accepted Jesus as my Lord and Savior!" What joy filled our hearts knowing he now had eternal life! As our relationship grew, J.P. ask us to pray for Carrie, his fiancé, back in China. Specifically, he asked us to pray it would become possible for her to come to America. Miraculously, our prayers were answered. Wedding bells rang, followed by a Chinese-style reception. We had the privilege of being a part of their special day.

Arriving at our home one day, J.P. and Carrie excitedly announced they were pregnant. Soon, they were blessed with a handsome baby boy. We were asked to name their son. The Chinese custom was to have the grandparents name the baby. Jack and I experienced the joy of being his American grandparents. We named this Chinese baby sporting a headful of jet-black hair Christopher Michael.

Another student we grew particularly close to was Carolyn Miwange, a beautiful and brilliant student from Kenya. Every Sunday morning for two years we picked her up at MIIS for church. This led to a running joke between us. She would lean over in church and whisper in our ears, "There is no one here my color." It was true then, not now.

She became valedictorian of her graduating class. Her entire family came from Kenya to attend her graduation. We spent a fascinating evening entertaining them in our home. Her father walked in our front door and handed Jack an exquisite, hand-carved African iron wood cane.

"Jack, this was carved by my Masai tribe," he proudly exclaimed. We treasure this very special gift. While we were together, Jack presented Carolyn with a photo of us with her whole family, attaching the moniker, "There's no one here our color!" This was just one of many of the enriching experiences we enjoyed through our involvement with ISI.

Christmas with our beloved friends, JP, Carrie, and Christopher.

Carolyn Miwange with her family at her her graduation from Monterey Institute of International Studies.

We began serving on the local ISI Advisory Council. Through that connection, we became acquainted with and grew to love the DePalatis family. Dale and his wife Caroline served alongside Kert and Lillie, eventually taking over the ministry when the older couple retired in early 2001.

While serving in a volunteer capacity with ISI, Dale was teaching English at Carmel High School and continues there at the time of this writing. Caroline, mother of their three children – Justin, Erika and Luke – served on ISI staff and led the ministry through the first decade of the 2000's.

Caroline also jumped into volunteer work at Carmel River School, the school across the street from our home, where eventually all three of her children attended and graduated. Luke, their youngest, arrived on the scene when Justin was in kindergarten and Erika attended preschool. I often took care of toddler Luke while Caroline volunteered across the street. Sometimes I would pick Justin and Erika up after school when obligations delayed Caroline. They became our beloved surrogate family on the Monterey Peninsula. Enjoying a big bowl of "Nana Sue's ice cream" became the thing the DePalatis children looked forward to whenever they visited.

Suddenly, seemingly out of the blue, an invitation arrived from Campus Crusade.

The DePalatis family in 2019: (left to right): Erika (21), Jacqueline (Justin's wife), Justin (23), Luke (18), Dale, and Caroline.

We worked with Campus Crusade's Jesus Video Project for many years, distributing this powerful film all over the world.

"Please come to Campus Crusade headquarters for the launching of the *Jesus Video Project*" the invite read.

Jack immediately became intrigued by the project. "Susie, we must go!"

It sounds like a perfect fit for us. "Jack, I do really want to go. I'll support you in what God is calling you to do. I simply don't have any extra time to do more than that, however." Community Bible Study had launched, and I was the teaching leader. This required study and writing a 45-minute teaching every week.

Following an inspiring presentation and challenge to distribute the *Jesus Video* far and wide, our attention turned to an easel with a map of the United States. The goal was to put one of these videos in every home in the United States. The leaders asked us to place a pin on our area of the country if we felt called to participate in this project. Jack and I, with our God-given zeal, walked hand-in-hand up to the map. We bowed together in prayer. As we proclaimed "amen," Jack placed a pin on the Monterey Peninsula, our new home.

Shortly after our return, Josh, the Southwest Area Director of Campus Crusade, called us.

"Jack and Sue, we would like for you to be the Area Directors of the *Jesus Video Project* for all of Monterey County!"

This was a *vastly* larger vision than just the Monterey Peninsula! With some prayer, we eventually agreed to meet the challenge. In spite of meeting with pastors and presenting the program again and again, we were never successful to launch a full countywide program.

We were part of the Ministerial Association of the Monterey Peninsula. This was a gathering of pastors and parachurch workers. Jack gave this group a presentation introducing them to the *Jesus Video Project*. They embraced the concept with dynamic enthusiasm. This was a historical event. It was the very first time 16 churches on the Monterey Peninsula ever united together for a single project! It was simply astounding and very gratifying to witness the unity of the different denominations.

With the growth of the internet and digitization, the *Jesus Video Project* became known as the *Jesus Film Project*. Now, a person with an internet connection just about anywhere on the planet can download the entire 60-minute film right on their cell phone! In DVD form and online, the *Jesus Film* is now available in more than 1700 languages! The goal is to have it translated in every language representing a population of over 50,000 people anywhere in the world.

The healing powers of the clean salt air improved my allergies to the point where I could pursue my dream of traveling. Now our travels were doubly joyous. We had the fantastic experience of distributing *The Jesus Video* Into the hands of eager and hungry hearts around the world. Many people would throw their arms around us with tears of gratitude when we placed the videos in their hands. We were overwhelmed by their reception. It was an incredibly gratifying experience.

The Jesus Film Project opened up new doors and new meaning for our overseas travel. Through a variety of trips all around the world, we could learn and experience the cultures of more than thirty-eight countries. This of course enriched us with a better understanding of this amazing world we live in. But we also had the opportunity to give hope to those we encountered along the way as we made available for free thousands of Jesus Videos and DVDs.

We found ourselves snorkeling around seven Galapagos Islands just four months after my first knee-replacement surgery. The entire experience felt miraculous. Our fellow tourists dubbed me the snorkeling queen. I never missed donning my wet suit and clamoring down the ropes into the zodiacs to dive in and view the breathtaking sea life. We hiked a different island each day. One day, we encountered the blue-footed boobies, a multitude of iguanas and many giant tortoises munching on grass. For us, exploring these fantastic islands was an otherworldly experience.

Over approximately 17 years, Jack and I soaked up the sights, sounds, life and culture of Peru, Ecuador, France, Spain, Italy, China, Turkey, Japan, Israel, Russia, Botswana, Zambia, Zimbabwe and South Africa. As a child, I had discovered a fascinating book about various African cultures in my stepfather's extensive personal library. The content mesmerized me. My heart ached to see the continent of Africa. Now it was actually happening!

We made an unexpected friend while traveling with Jim and Jill in the Galapagos Islands!

Jack and I exploring Macchu Picchu in Peru.

A safari in Africa was high on my bucket list. Landing in Cape Town, we caught the fog settling over Table Mountain like a tablecloth, a truly breathtaking sight transporting my memory to Kevin, our AFS student from long ago. I could almost hear his voice, with its distinctive South African accent, describe this scenic phenomenon to us. Kevin was a charismatic ambassador for his homeland.

Kevin's family home stood in Johannesburg. I prayed I could connect with his family still living there. Miraculously, it happened. We spent a treasured afternoon and evening with his mother, Mindy, and his sister, Anna Louise. Mindy came bearing piles of photos of Kevin, wife Suzanne, and their family of now twelve children.

At 11:00 pm, our hotel phone rang abruptly, startling us out of our sleep. Wondering who might call at such an hour, I managed a "Hello."

"Mum?" My heart leapt, "Kevin!" A voice I hadn't heard for thirty years floated across the wires, all the way from London. My expectations and anticipations of a lifetime had just doubled. You simply can't out-give God, can you? I immediately shot up a praise to God for making this possible.

Leaving Johannesburg, we flew to Hoedspruit, for a five-day African safari. Our bus took us on a wild, bumpy road to Thorny Bush Lodge. We enjoyed appetizing meals in an open-air thatched-roof pavilion while monkeys frolicked on the roof. They frequently leaped upon the serving table, snatching a loaf of bread and scampering away. A gun-bearing attendant escorted us constantly.

We climbed in the Land Rover with our driver and armed attendant seated on an extended front seat. We were in awe as we looked out at the wild animals in their natural habitat – baboons, monkeys, rhinoceros, impalas, monitor lizards, warthogs, antelope, greater kudus, water bucks, leopards, cape buffalos, zebras, rhinos, and elephants. The guides cautioned us to never make eye contact with the animals.

One particular morning, rain began to fall. Our Land Rover sat parked near a pride of lions. They were lazily lounging on and around each other. As it started to rain, one male with a magnificent mane slowly rose and lumbered into a bush close to us. As we watched him settle down, probably just six feet from us, it happened! He turned and looked directly at us. And moments later, we were eyeball-to- eyeball!

Help! Who would he attack first?!? Our reckless sporting spirit suddenly vaporized. Our driver calmed us with these reassuring words. "Never fear, he has already had his morning feast." That's the reason they were lazily lounging when we came upon them. And they never seemed afraid of us at all!

We could observe up close the stately zebras, prides of lions, and a barking cheetah. I even referred to him as

Our safari guides told us not to stare directly into a lion's eyes... too late!

This photo of a cheetah that I took on our safari is one of my favorites!

my barking cheetah because I snapped a photo of him I'm particularly proud of. It stands out among the 1,500 I took during this excursion in Africa. (And this is pre-digital camera days.) This cheetah is my forever screen saver on my computer. Each time I turn on my computer he instantly transports me to the wild, exciting bush of Africa. Seeing his huge biceps makes me realize how easily he can run sixty miles an hour.

Did I mention photography, especially of nature, is one of my hobbies?

In Zimbabwe, we stayed at the Livingston Hotel overlooking the Zambezi River. We felt the spray and mist from the famous Victoria Falls. Against its magnificent, crashing force, a giant perpetual rainbow stretched. Monkeys cavorted around everywhere. One evening, we sat sipping wine and munching snacks by the river, the roar of the crashing falls enveloping us. Suddenly, a monkey dropped from an overhanging branch. We jumped, startled and surprised as he landed smack dab in the middle of our table. In a flash he grabbed our snacks and scurried away.

Visiting a nearby village gave us an up-close view of how impoverished the surrounding villages were, however. Preschool children came up to us, holding our hands as we toured their village. Branches and mud were the building materials of their homes. One woman appeared to be the sole adult there. She was stirring slurry, a gruel-like porridge in a small black iron pot over an open fire. My heart ached when I saw the children, wishing somehow I could offer them a life with less deprivation.

Jack and I at Victoria Falls.

Many of our fulfilling travels were with professors from the University of California, Berkeley, who would educate us as we explored new places. We have traveled the continents of our world for over thirty years together. The education, experiences and visuals have made us wealthier than any billionaire. These experiences fulfilled my travel desires beyond my wildest dreams.

The year was 2010. Jack kept on telling me, "Susie, I just don't feel good at all." We began consulting a number of different physicians to figure out what might be going on. Our primary care doctor suggested we try a different climate.

We spent a month in Rancho Mirage, California, thinking the warmer weather might help. But Jack's health continued to decline. Upon our return, we consulted a pulmonologist.

At the time, we had an impending trip planned to Russia. We agreed, if his current doctor indicated he was well enough to go, we would go. Jack's pulmonologist, Dr. Pogemeyer, answered our query in the positive. "Go. Please go! In fact, I wish you needed me to go with you!"

Very reluctantly, Jack agreed to go on this trip. His stipulation was, "Susie, you must take care of all the details of the trip." That meant setting up our frequent flyer miles we used for our plane reservations. There were also detailed tour arrangements to finalize with the University of California alumni travel office.

On all our previous overseas treks Jack, with his efficient organizational skills along with his devotion to detail, made our trips run like perfect clockwork.

"Yes," I responded. "I will try my best to accomplish these tasks. At the same time my heart was heavy as I questioned this shocking ultimatum.

A person of great precision and detail – dotting all the i's and crossing all the t's – that would describe my husband, Jack Wulfmeyer. It was completely out of character for him to ask me, a creative, broad-brush person to take charge of all the details for our trip to Russia. Troubling questions continually swirled through my mind.

Visions of seeing some of Russia's treasures helped me, by God's grace, to persevere. Challenged by Jack's imperative, I procured plane tickets coordinating with our UC Berkeley alumni tour. Wheelchair transportation was easily arranged for every airport terminal.

On July 16th, 2010 we were jetting across the sea landing at the Moscow airport. There we connected with our tour group. Boarding the private tour bus to our boat "The Blue Voyage," we were on our way. This UC Berkeley tour was entitled "Peter The Great." Each of us on the tour received a thick, fascinating book full of facts on Russia. Informative lectures on board happened every afternoon.

The riverboat trip between Moscow and St. Petersburg afforded Jack extra rest. On days he didn't feel well, he

Jack and I in Russia, our last overseas trip together.

opted out of some land excursions. Early on, I realized I had a choice to make. I could privately mourn over all the adventures we could no longer enjoy together, or I could choose to let go and let God take care of the situation. I chose the latter.

And, as I let go, my loving Lord surrounded me with a group of engaging, fun gals on the tour. We enjoyed our time together viewing the many historic Russian sites. It did seem strange to me how, on our 39th trip together as a couple, I was only sharing part of it with Jack. My heart wondered, *Lord, is this the new path you have for us?*

In St. Petersburg, I felt especially dismayed when Jack missed experiencing our fabulous tour of the Hermitage. The enormous Amber Room "dubbed the 8th wonder of the world" contained amber and gold panels that adorned the room from floor to ceiling. Those golden jewel-encrusted walls with their tons of gemstones dazzle and amaze my memory to this very day.

After a day of rest, Jack was able to attend a performance of "Giselle" by the Royal Ballet Academy.

Entering through the ornate doors of the theatre, we were treated like royalty. Jack and I were actually seated in Catherine the Great's favorite seat just behind the orchestra. I am still in awe of that "dream come true" evening.

Returning home from Russia, I was broadsided by Jack's declaration, "I am not traveling abroad ever again!" My hope was that, after this smooth-sailing trip to Russia, he would desire to continue traveling. I was not ready to cease our amazing life of adventurous foreign travel. A fire burned in my heart to continue gaining knowledge and experience, and to offer hope to people around the world. We always spread the Good News of Jesus Christ with gifts of the *Jesus* DVD to people in the locations we visited.

Jack was adamant, however.

"No more traveling 'across the pond' for me. It's just too much hassle. I can't walk well enough. I can't hear well enough. It's too much for me to cope with. My going through security with an artificial hip, being patted down, making sure I have the proper bottles of medicine in my carry-on case and everything that entails meeting government security regulations is just too hard. I'm just too old."

12

Twilight Reflections

Evening Primrose
Eternal love

My heart ached as puzzling questions whirled through my mind. *Why was Jack so firm in his absolute refusal to travel? What was causing his attitudes and actions to change?* Gazing at him across our breakfast table one morning, even his countenance had noticeably changed.

At Jack's opthamologist appointment, his doctor asked him if he felt well. "No," he replied, not skipping a beat. His doctor urged him to see a neurologist. The results of the appointment with this neurologist shocked us. After some tests, his diagnosis was Parkinson's disease.

Parkinson's Disease, or "PD," was like a foreign word to us. All we knew about it was as singular symptom, that of trembling hands. Jack definitely didn't show any signs of that.

Our first step was to Google it. After doing diligence in reading through a number of reports, I began to understand the varied signs of this debilitating disease.

Jack was experiencing loss of smell. He also exhibited more restrained facial expressions and a faltering gait. He became less able to process my conversations, and this haunted me. Often he would state, "I don't know what you are talking about!" His handwriting soon became microscopic. These were some of the harbingers of Jack's Parkinson's.

In fact, Parkinson's is considered a "boutique illness" in that it manifests itself differently in each individual it invades. We learned there are over 70 types of PD.

We continued to search for all the information we could get our hands on about this mysterious stranger invading our lives. We both knew the New Testament Bible verse, "You shall know the truth and the truth will set you free" (John 8:32). Learning there were five medical centers in the U.S. devoted to Parkinson's research with one located in San Jose, California, we quickly contacted them for an appointment. The first available one was in six months. In the meantime we were consulting with our local neurologist.

As we shared with others Jack's diagnosis, we were

shocked by the number of friends and acquaintances who had grappled with the disease somehow in their or a loved one's life. They would frequently relay their experiences with the disease.

"Oh, that's a horrible disease," was a common refrain. Some suggested I enroll Jack into a day program, so I could have some free time.

"Sue, you must get away for a weekend once a month," one friend advised.

We learned of a local monthly meeting of Parkinson's patients and their caregivers. They had monthly speakers to inform and help us through this maze. The first time we attended, the speaker had canceled abruptly. The organizers seated us at two separate tables, one for caregivers and one for patients.

At the caregivers table, we were to share our journey with the disease. I listened to a gentleman tell about his wife. The past year he rushed her to the hospital three times with broken bones after falling. University of California San Francisco's (UCSF) medical information included warnings about how PD patients could simply fall backwards as they walk along. Jack, sitting with the group afflicted with Parkinson's, listened to even more horror stories. We both realized then, it was unfortunate there was no speaker. Kind of like baptism by fire, it proved a very alarming and discouraging experience.

One of the symptoms of Parkinson's is a sense of acute stress. Indeed, this was increasing exponentially for Jack. Keeping everything simple was paramount. I learned how important it would be from now on to pay keen attention to the timing when introducing and discussing new events. This would help with Jack's difficulty in coping with unknown situations. At this time, he was quite lucid and well aware of his slow deterioration.

After the long six-month wait, we went to San Jose for our appointment. To keep this trip as easy as possible, I arranged for us to stay the night before his appointment in a motel close to the Parkinson's Center. The next morning after our fitful night's rest, Jack was admitted to the Center and his battery of tests began.

Dr. Liang, our assigned doctor, was thorough and encouraging. She pinpointed Jack's memory and mobility issues. The doctor emphasized the importance of increased physical activity for physical and mental acuity. This program would help fight the dopamine damaging his brain. She informed us we were very fortunate to live close to an excellent physical therapist specializing in Parkinson's Disease, Jeannine Yip.

Now, having gained some knowledge and understanding, and armed with our faith and dependence on our Lord, the Great Physician, we were beginning to get a grasp of what this new path of life would mean for us.

Several times each week I drove Jack to Marina, a 30-minute trip, where the Community Hospital of the Monterey Peninsula's Wellness Center was located. We learned a lot about the disease during Jack's first dozen sessions with Jeannine. It was comforting to feel better equipped for our road ahead.

Jack and I were astounded when Jeanine recommended we consult a speech therapist. Sitting in her office, she surprised us by saying, "After listening to my analysis, Jack, you decide whether or not you want to sign up for my speech program. If you choose to do the set exercises I provide you, you must commit totally to following the regime. Otherwise, there is no point in wasting your or my good time."

There was a key sentence in her presentation that convinced both of us Jack should accept her challenge.

"Jack, these exercises will help reprogram your brain to circumvent the area damaged by the dopamine formed by Parkinson's." Wow, we were so encouraged and excited by that statement! We had observed that type of miraculous healing in a dear young friend. She suffered major brain damage in a horrific automobile accident. We witnessed her gradual healing as different parts of her brain took over the permanently damaged areas.

"Yes, yes, sign us up!"

I say "us" because Jack was no longer driving. And this was our journey, together. On this new pathway, Jack's day-to-day goal would be to exercise the brain and body. My goal would be to encourage and help him in every way I possibly could. I refused to be entangled in the web of anxious confusion or worry. My choice was not to listen to the deafening noise of the world. Listening to my all-knowing Lord was the path I chose. Immediately, I claimed Philippians 4:13, *"I can do all things through Christ who strengthens me."*

Our lifestyle changed dramatically. His steps continued to falter, his reasoning processes became more difficult, and his memory began to dim. There would be no more traveling abroad.

With his keen mind, Jack was aware of his increasing limitations. He was greatly concerned about my assuming our financial affairs. "Sue, how are you going to pay our bills?" he questioned.

"Oh, that's easy, Jack. I will go back to handling them the way I did when I was a widow. I wrote checks and mailed them off each month."

"No, you need to learn to do our banking online," he insisted. My confidence level in doing that on a scale of 1–10 was about a 2! My young friends said, "No, Sue, you can't go back to paying bills the old-fashioned way! You can learn to handle the bills online."

Taking a deep breath, I once again claimed our Lord's promise in Phillipians 4:13, "I can do all things through Christ who strengthens me."

That day came when I declared, "Jack, I will pay our bills and handle our finances online." I instantly saw his countenance clear, as if a huge weight had been lifted from his shoulders. Immediately, my numbers guy – you know, the one with the MBA in Finance – began to teach me, a total neophyte, how to handle all our finances electronically. I discovered that even at 80 years of age I could still learn.

He was so loving and patient with me. Still, the task was daunting. I felt like I had earned my MBA by the time he taught me all his financial processes! The scariest part for me in the beginning was doing all the banking online. The words of one of my favorite Christian songs kept running through my head: *Trust and obey for there's no other way, to be happy in Jesus, but to trust and obey.*

Now, many years later, it's all second nature to me. It's amazing how a giant mountain can morph into a miniscule molehill when you put your trust in an all-knowing God.

Jack could no longer physically or mentally be the talented fix-it person I had always depended on. Gone were the days of my calling, "Oh, Jack! I've cut a drip line in the garden," or, "Oh, Jack! I need computer help," or, "Oh, Jack! The kitchen door is sticking."

My Jack had always sprung into instant action when I called. I quickly realized how bountifully blessed I was. Now it was my turn to give back. I knew of my God's faithfulness to care for me. I had a mini flashback to the day of my personal encounter with Him on that dusty Illinois country road when I was four years old.

The Bible verse I had claimed for my life was Romans 8:28: *"And we know that in all things God works for the good of those who love him, who have been called according to His purpose."* That verse gave me such blessed assurance! I had personally witnessed its absolute truth in my life. And the many miracles of God I have experienced I knew, with confidence, would indeed continue to happen, for we have a miracle-working God.

Now I needed to pray and listen to the Lord's specific directions for my next step. I had always claimed a person could have many careers in a single life. My new profession at age 78 was to become a caregiver. Clearly, this was God's new call on my life. I committed to giving Jack as much love and support as I was capable of giving. My desire was to excel in this new career God had planned for me.

In the next year, as we were adapting to living with Parkinson's disease, one of God's many miracles occurred. We reported Jack's increasing memory problems to his neurologist. He suggested we try a drug called Namenda on a trial basis. This treatment proved so successful that Jack was able to recover some of his former skills. He was also able to advise me when I needed business advice. Our communication with each other improved. I burst with thanksgiving for this dramatic change in Jack.

Soon Jack put into action the Bible verse James 5:14, "Is any one of you sick? He should call the elders of the church to gather and pray over him." The very next Sunday following Jack's call to our church, five elders of our church gathered around Jack. They anointed him with oil; we all laid hands on him and prayed for his healing.

The many instances of Jesus' healing in the New Testament of the Bible came in different ways and forms. The verse just preceding James 5:14 says "Is any one of you in trouble? He should pray. Is any one of you happy? Let him sing songs of praise (James 5:13)." We kept praising and praying for God's continuing direction each day.

Parkinson's Disease feels like riding a roller coaster. One day will be great, filling us with hope. The next day will be the pits, bringing discouragement. Through this experience, we both learned "to be content in all things," like the Apostle Paul in Philippians 4:11.

We walked hand-in-hand, in spirit, together, committed to following every avenue to improve our lives mentally and physically with the joint challenges of PD and old age. Jack faithfully did his many physical and speech exercises. His activities kept diminishing, however. Our daily walk went from six blocks just to one block. He no longer was able to go to the gym, attend church or the Carmel Rotary Club. His frequent falls demanded he use a walker at all times.

Our stairs became dangerous for Jack to manage. His move downstairs transformed our den into his "man cave." Jack's new digs housed his mechanical bed and his reclining lift chair. His life went from the world to his man cave. Jack became a voracious reader. I invited couples for afternoon tea to keep Jack interacting with people. These times were a gift to both of us.

Suddenly one of Jack's eyes became very painful. Our opthamologist informed us Jack had a torn retina. This was caused by the slowing down of his blinking reflex. Miraculously, after undergoing eye surgery, his eye healed. For the rest of his life, I would apply an antibiotic salve to that eye.

Every evening we tuned into the news so we could pray for world and local events. That was followed by *Jeopardy* to kick off our mentally challenging games, and then *Wheel of Fortune*. Playing our repertoire of board and card games – Scrabble, Stack Scrabble, Mexican Train, Rummikub, and King's Court – no longer happened. We read about travel adventures rather than doing them ourselves. Our world travel narrowed to the relatively small area of the Monterey Peninsula.

Professionals counseled me to remember to take care of myself in my role as caregiver. I heard to their advice: "You must take breaks from this new job. You need to get away once in awhile." But, wanting to be the best caregiver possible, I chose to listen to God for guidance and decisions. The peace he gave me proved sufficient. Even though I would get weary, I didn't sense I needed much time away.

The journey was so arduous at times, the walk often plodding and heavy. Though the path was difficult and the scenery often dull, I knew my God had a sparkling surprise just around each and every bend. My heart's desire was to simply live up to God's vision for me. Knowing His blessed assurance and my trust in Him gave me the confidence to know I could.

It became abundantly clear to me how God had prepared me for such a time as this. At age five, He gave me my role model: Grandmother Gray, so full of joy as she cared for her husband, my grandfather, with his Alzheimer's disease. I marveled at her peace and contentment as she went through her busy days. Now, I was able to relate to her spirit. Like her, my days were very busy. My daughter Holly exclaimed, "Mom, you are working harder than I am!" Maybe so. At the same time, it was a privilege and a joy to be wonderfully weary caring for my loving husband.

It became clear to me we needed more help caring for our home and garden. I called it God's perfect timing.

The Carmel Foundation, a senior citizen's center, had just announced the inception of The Monterey Bay Village. This countywide organization was created to help senior citizens stay in their own homes, and is part of a larger, nationwide network.

The Monterey Bay Village has over sixty screened volunteers waiting for our call for help. Vetted contractors give seniors a ten percent reduction in their fees.

My love of gardening is as ardent today as the day I discovered its magical pull for me. Oops, I managed to cut a drip line while digging in my new butterfly bush! There would be Jeff from The Village, answering my call for help. At the same time, my computer might have had a serious glitch. There would be Dick, coming right over to help me. I would feel as if Jack needed a guy to talk with. Put in a call to The Village and, before we knew it, Rich would be knocking at the door, so they could have a man-to-man talk. This is just a picture of what The Monterey Bay Village looks like. I even had the privilege of being among those chosen to share the program on our local television station!

Jack's ability to do things for himself diminished day by day. I soon needed to dress and undress him. He remained mobile, with his walker, for a little while. He was becoming more frail as well. Pressure wounds began developing. His doctor sent him to the hospital's wound center. I would take him there once a week. They instructed me to feed him a high-protein diet. I purchased cases of Ensure Plus, a drink high in protein, containing all the daily requirements of minerals and vitamins. I also bought a case of Protein Plus.

The Visiting Nurses Association came two times a week to treat Jack's wounds.

I endeavored to cook the very best meals to meet his health needs. He loved scrambled eggs, so I would stir heavy whipping cream into two eggs, then fortify them with five different fresh vegetables, lightly browned in olive oil. Then I'd top them with a variety of cheeses. Each morning I would serve them with sausage and tater tots. I replaced his favorite V8 breakfast drink with protein-rich Ensure Plus. When he ate and drank all his breakfast, I believed he was off to a good nutritional start for the day. We enjoyed each other's company while eating breakfast, sitting in front of our fireplace. Following breakfast, I would read two of our favorite devotionals, "My Utmost for His Highest" by Oswald Chambers, and "Jesus Calling" by Sarah Young. Jack would follow up by reading Scripture, and we would end with prayers of thanksgiving and requests for our missionaries and friends.

In spite of enriching his diet, Jack kept getting thinner. Getting him out of bed proved increasingly challenging. While the world seemed to keep speeding up, we were getting slower. Often it would be 10:30 or 11:00 am before Jack started his morning regime of exercises. Juggling doctors appointments, wound center days, visiting nurse times – all the while aiming to keep Jack's routine stable – proved a distinct challenge. Jack never wanted me to leave him. He always wanted to know where I was in the house. I was simply exhausted! The time had arrived for some outside help.

It was now time to open the manila folder I had labeled "caregivers." When Jack was diagnosed with PD, I knew this time would eventually come. Every time I had heard about a caregiver, I would drop a card with their information in that manila folder. As I opened it up, I knew whom I would call first. I said a short prayer. "Lord, may it be your will to send us Lela Simi."

I knew Lela personally. She is a dedicated Tongan Christian caregiver. For 12 years she took care of my friend Sue's mother. I had connected with her recently. She sang with a local Tongan choir. They gloriously sang Christian songs for a memorial service I gave for a dear friend.

While calling her, I sent up a quick arrow prayer, my favorite instant request knowing Jesus is always listening. My heart skipped a beat as I heard her familiar voice answer, "Hello?"

"Oh, Lela, it is a blessing to hear your voice!" I exclaimed. After our mutual reactions to reuniting, I inquired, "Lela, do you have any free days to be Jack's caregiver?" She quickly responded that she did. I was so grateful for this response that tears splashed out of my eyes.

Three days a week, Lela would greet us each morning with her cheery voice, "I'm here!" She was a breath of fresh air for both Jack and me. On her first day with Jack, she told me, "Sue, I want to keep busy." Lela loved ironing, folding clothes, polishing silverware, and gardening. Indeed, she was truly an angel sent to lighten my work load. My thankfulness for all her help knew no bounds.

Jack called this stage of our life "the hard season." It

definitely was that, so challenging as the advanced stages of PD buffeted us on all sides. But, through God's grace, we experienced renewed peace and inner joy along the way. Though our daily routine became quite humdrum, we also became so extraordinarily thankful and full of praise for all the helpful angels he sent our way.

I was continually amazed by Jack's appreciation of me and his mental processing of advice I would challenge him with. For example, I would ask for his wisdom as to whether I should update my old computer or simply purchase a new one. While it would take him awhile to process my questions, I was so grateful when he was able to respond. He never complained and was almost always compliant. He continually told me how much he loves and appreciates me. His speech became more garbled. Often I had to ask him to repeat something several times. This was the only time he showed any sign of frustration.

Yes, PD forced me to ask him endless times to repeat what he had said. Even with his years of commitment to his speech exercises, PD slowly robbed him of clear speech. Eventually, he could no longer swallow automatically. His saliva would just sit in his mouth. This would cause his speech to become garbled. Fortunately, he wouldn't object to my saying multiple times a day, "Honey, take a deep breath, swallow hard and then tell me what you just said."

With the diagnosis of PD, Jack's typical approach to challenges would be, "I can't do this." I would let this go in one ear and out the other because I knew he could manage to do it. Sometimes, I would have to insist that he do something. Case in point, on one Saturday night our "Intrepid group" of five couples would meet every month at our home. Together we have feasted, fellowshipped, shared Scripture and prayer, praises and requests, for 18 years. When I called Jack to the dinner table, he responded, "I can't do it." I took a deep breath and simply told him, "Jack, push your chair's lift button, grab your walker, and come with me!" These are times I needed to push him. Interacting with others was so beneficial for him and, after all, he enjoyed it.

Once seated at the table, Jack would usually say grace or, if not, he would ask someone else to do it. He would enter into and enjoy the evening. That particular Saturday he surprised us all by closing our time together with a deep, insightful prayer. We all were so blessed by his clear articulation.

During this season, Jack and I were humbled at how God continuously poured out His love and care on us. Jack would often cough and choke from not swallowing enough. It would be especially troublesome at night. Lela suggested, "Sue, give him soda to drink." Indeed, the effervescence would help him. He would drink a glass of this sparkling water while taking his bedtime pills. It slightly reduced his coughing at night. Lela's 30 years of caregiving experience helped us in so many ways.

The roller coaster kept us going up and down. At one point, Jack's appetite improved and he gained seven pounds. Every week for six months I would take Jack to the hospital wound center. His wound doctor told us his six pressure wounds would probably never heal. But, miraculously, all six of his pressure wounds healed! His doctor was astounded. We told him we believe in the power of prayer. Our doctor finally acknowledged the power of prayer in this process.

With the healing of his pressure wounds, Jack's strength started returning. Once again, he was able to take short walks in our neighborhood. A few years earlier, the Carmel Foundation had loaned us a walker for outside, one with a seat. I had already returned it. But then we needed it again.

Rejoicing with Lela as I related this miracle, she told me, "Sue, I have a walker with a seat in my garage. I will bring it tomorrow."

Lela arrived the next day with an almost-new walker. She informed me this was a short-term loan. She would be shipping it to Tonga for her aunt. "Sue, do check with the Carmel Foundation. They may have a similar one."

Arriving at the Foundation, I contacted Kari. She was in charge of their free medical equipment. Her eyes sparkled with excitement as she heard our need for an outside walker.

"Sue, we just received a top-of-the-line walker." Wheeling it into the cafe where I sat working at my computer, she announced, "Surprise!"

One of the cafe visitors exclaimed, "That must be the Cadillac of walkers!"

Kari responded, "I think it's more like the Tesla of walkers!"

In less than a week, we went from no walker to two of them! The Tesla had high handles to help Jack from slumping. It fit the exact description one of Jack's daughters, Cindy, had called to tell us about a week earlier.

Some would call this all a coincidence. We would call it God's perfect, abundant provision. Our Lord promises he will provide our every need. My heart fills with off-the-charts joy every time I experience God's love and care afresh. I find it to be a glorious affirmation of my faith. His provision allowed us a season where we could take "Tessie" out twice a day to walk around the block – a breath of fresh air for Jack and me in so many ways.

Sparkling Interlude

In the midst of all the ups and downs of Jack's Parkinson's journey, an entirely unexpected opportunity opened up for us. It involved a knock on our door, a phone call, and a request from a crew of Hollywood filmmakers (50 in all) to visit our home and yard.

One Sunday afternoon I opened the front door and a pleasant looking gentleman greeted me with an inquiry.

"May I take several pictures of your home?"

I instantly responded, "You are welcome to do so! Thank you for asking. I see people taking pictures of our home and yard all the time, but they never ask our permission."

"Well, I do have a special reason," he continued.

"A film company is looking for a particular house for an upcoming production. Here is my card." Thanking him as I closed the door, red flags of caution whizzed through my mind.

The Monterey County Film Commissioner, Karen Nordstrand, had recently presented a program to my sorority alumni group. Immediately, I called Karen. She confirmed, to my great relief, "Yes, this man is legit."

Shortly after Karen's confirmation the phone rang. "Hello, Mrs. Wulfmeyer. I'm Jere Newton, and I am the local Locations/Production Liaison for a film company interested in potentially using your home in a production. May I come visit you? I have been asked to check out the area around your front door as a possible filming location."

Opening our front door, I encountered a tall, vivacious redhead.

"Hi, I'm Jere Newton. Here is my card." With extreme politeness and consideration, she asked, "May I just take one step into your home? I've been asked to take a photo looking at your garden." I certainly had no problem with that request.

Two days later, Jere called again. "Sue, could we have permission to bring fifty Hollywood production people to your home next Monday? We are considering the possibility of using your home in the filming of an HBO series, entitled *Big Little Lies*. It is based on the book *Big Little Lies* authored by Liane Moriarty. Your home is under consideration for Reese Witherspoon's beach house in Carmel."

Suddenly Jack and I were catapulted into Hollywood

film culture. Monday dawned sunny and bright, bringing that busload of film producers along with the director, Jean-Marc Vallee.

They liked what they saw. The director requested a picture taken of him and me together. Turning to me he asked, "Sue, would you consider appearing in one scene?"

Instant amazement shot through my mind as I replied, "Why, yes!" I, a Hollywood neophyte, had suddenly been catapulted into a Hollywood movie scene. I was incredulous. *One can always have another career* is an idea I have often believed.

Of course, I was concerned about how Jack would be affected by all this. He required a set routine as we grappled with his physical decline. We prayed together and, with our Assistant Pastor's prayer and guidance, along with advice from well-informed movie buffs, we came to believe we should sign that Hollywood contract My private prayer was "Dear Lord may this obvious disruption bless Jack in ways we can't possibly envision right now."

The process of transforming our home into a beach house stretched our imagination to its outer limits. *How could our two-story house, one that looks like it belongs in Connecticut, become a beach house?* We soon learned the true meaning of a Hollywood production.

The day dawned bright and sunny. Let the show begin! Fourteenth Avenue quickly became a movie production lot. The trash hauler arrived, along with the Porta-Potty unit. A huge, bright blue crane, along with a large transport truck filled with building supplies, made its station in front of our

My daughters, Jill and Holly, with Reese Witherspoon and I during the filming of Big Little Lies outside our home-turned-beach house!

home. Next came a large van stocked with flats of bedding plants, bushes, trees, peacock-blue pots and window boxes for landscaping. Then came the tall street lights, walkway lights, spot lights and decorative garden lights.

Next, the crew, along with 24/7 guards, arrived. In addition, painters, builders, electricians, landscapers, furniture movers, and designers rounded out the team. A buzz of excitement filled the air for the two weeks they were readying our property for the filming.

On the actual day of filming, the sun broke through the coastal fog in all its brilliance. The director was pleased to find everything in order.

My daughters Jill and Holly along with son-in-law Jim arrived right at the time of filming. They weren't going to miss a minute of this once-in-a-lifetime experience. The phone rang.

"Hello Sue. This is Jere. We expect film stars Reese Witherspoon and Adam Scott to arrive in 15 minutes."

Moments later, Reese stepped through our entryway and into our home with her wardrobe lady. She greeted us with a warm and gracious smile.

We arranged chairs in the dining room archway. From there, our five family members were able to meet the stars and view the indoor filming.

Soon after, Director Jean-Marc and his assistant stepped in. Immediately, the actors and crew took their positions and the filming began. Jean-Marc turned to his assistant and must have spied me sitting next to Jack. At once he stopped, put down his camera, and walked over to

Jack. Holding out his hand to shake Jack's, he exclaimed, "Thank you very much for allowing us to use your home for this film." He chatted with us a little longer. We were very impressed by his kind outreach to us in the middle of filming a scene.

When Reese entered the room, she spent quite a lot of time with us. And she insisted on having our pictures taken with her. Everyone graciously signed our purchased copy of the book "Big Little Lies."

This whole sparkling process was so filled with unanticipated blessings. We were sad when, the next day, the crew arrived to meticulously restore our home to its original design.

Saying goodbye, I presented each one with a bag containing the Jesus DVD and a homemade chocolate chip cookie. As I handed them the bag I said, "This bag holds a token of my love as well as a DVD of perfect love for you."

I waved goodbye as the last truck left for Hollywood. Slowly walking toward our home, I watched the pebbled path fade away to bricks. Gazing at our Connecticut look-alike home, the Carmel cottage also faded away. For the two weeks this all lasted, it seemed to me like a dream. Now we awakened and life returned to its usual challenges.

Sparkling moments with shooting stars suddenly

appeared again. The airing of the six episodes of *Big Little Lies* proved hugely popular worldwide. Hollywood decided to produce a second series. This series required writing an original script. Several Oscar-winning women took the top roles. In addition to Reese Witherspoon, the new series starred Meryl Streep, Nicole Kidman, Laura Dern and Shailene Woodley.

The new director was Andrea Arnold from England. To my amazement, Jere called to inform us they were interested in using our home for another scene.

The team arrived. It was a blessed, bountiful moment of warm greetings and hugs. Greg Alpert, the Locations Manager, arrived from Los Angeles and presented me with a DVD of the first series. The crew checked out different locations in our home for possible scenes on three occasions. Unfortunately, this time the scene, script, and setting just didn't come together.

We continued our journey ahead, clinging to God on the roller coaster ride of Parkinson's Disease. Grappling with late-stage PD, Jack persevered with his walker and fed himself as much as he could. He would sleep frequently, even as I worked with him on his morning exercises and as we'd watch TV together in the early evening.

The signs of fall filled the air as I prepared for Jack's

90th birthday on September 9th that year. God's still, quiet voice told me this would likely be his last birthday. I sent out invitations to the family. The theme for his party was "Tribute, Toast, or Roast (or all three)!"

When the day arrived, interwoven stories triggered both tears and laughter. Jack sat at the table for three hours thoroughly enjoying and reminiscing as the family shared. He was the one there to be blessed, but I think we were the most blessed watching and listening to him.

Musing how to make our 41st anniversary on October 21st that year a particularly special one, I found myself having a mini-flashback moment. Our wedding anniversaries had all been creative adventures, all orchestrated by Jack. There were times he instructed me to pack an overnight bag. He would whisk me off for a romantic weekend. Another time, he instructed me to wear my wedding dress for our dinner date out. That time, at dinner he announced he was taking me to our church. Walking into the church, I gasped in amazement; he had replicated our wedding day, complete with flowers, music, and a complete ceremony!

Pondering how I could make this anniversary special, I felt I faced an insurmountable task. Then God reminded me His grace is sufficient for everything. I set up a table with Jack's favorite red rose from our garden. Next, I set out our wedding album. Out of our refrigerator, I pulled a tiny bottle of pink sparkling wine and poured it into small sherry glasses. It tasted just like the crackling rose wine we had served at our wedding reception. We sipped it as I read our wedding vows. It was to be our last anniversary celebration

Jack with Pastor Geoff.

on this earth.

For some time now, one Monday each month had become the time when our faithful, beloved Pastor Geoff Buck and Jack would enjoy lunch together. For several years, I dropped Jack off at their favorite restaurant. Now it had become too difficult for Jack to go out to eat. Pastor Geoff came faithfully to our home. I would serve them lunch and then leave them to enjoy each others' company.

This particular Monday, as Jack tried to get to the table, he collapsed. I called 911. Soon he was rushed to the Emergency Room. Six hours later, he was placed in the Intensive Care Unit. The doctor informed us Jack had a massive infection in his gallbladder. Two days later he had surgery.

Even though he was very thin and weak, Jack never lost his wit. One day the nurse came in his room and asked, "Mr. Wulfmeyer, how are you feeling?"

He turned to her and said, "If I was feeling good, I wouldn't be here!"

A week and a half later he was sent to rehab. Even though they pureed his food, he was having difficulty swallowing anything.

The Hospice nurse came in Jack's room to present their home care program to me. As she finished, she remarked, "Mrs. Wulfmeyer, I will come back tomorrow after you have had time to think about this."

I was bursting with gratitude knowing this was the answer to my prayers to bring Jack back home. I responded immediately, "Where do I sign? I don't need to think about it!"

Our beloved Lela, Jack's part-time caregiver, was on her way to visit her family in Tonga. Another caregiver, Michael, had taken her place temporarily and immediately endeared himself to us. Right away, Michael and I transformed Jack's man cave into a hospital room, complete with a bed and all the necessities a hospital patient would need. It was two weeks before Christmas. MIchael helped me decorate our home for Christmas and took excellent care of Jack. I dubbed him "Michael the Archangel." He truly was God's gift to us.

On my birthday, December 17th, my beloved Jack was able to tell me "Happy Birthday!" three times. Those were the last words he was able to vocalize. Every day during that next week and a half, we would hug and tell each other, "I love you." Jack was unable to vocalize, but I could hear the words through his eyes. His lips often mouthed the words he could no longer utter.

The peace of God enveloped us on our last two days on earth together. Whispering God's words, "Let go, Love" at 10:00 pm. just five days before Christmas, my beloved Jack went to be with his Lord and Savior Jesus Christ.

All our family gathered together to celebrate the birthday of Jesus. Our home was filled with the spirit of Jack's love. I remain enveloped in God's and in Jack's love to this day.

Envisioning Jack's entrance into heaven and meeting my mother, I wrote the reflection contained in Appendix 2 at the end of this book.

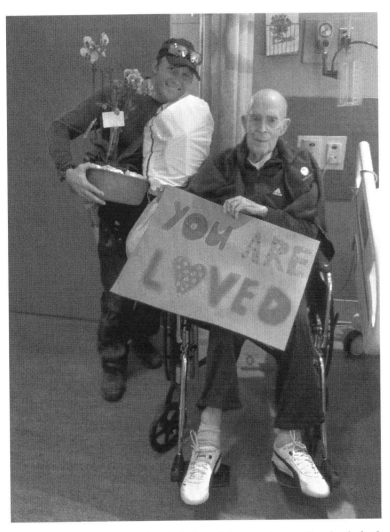

The last photo taken of Jack before his passing, after he left the hospital to return to home care, with his caretaker Michael. Jack was and is so loved.

Basking in God's eternal love and that of Jack's, I found myself surrounded by stunning flowers sent in his memory. The multitudes of flowers, cards, hugs, and donations in Jack's memory carried me on angel's wings of comfort and inner joy during this profound season of loss.

I found myself so thankful Jack was now released from his Parkinson's diseased body, and free in a new, heavenly body.

I do frequently feel like half of me is gone, however. Jack and I were truly one in our spirit and flesh. Ephesians 5:31 says, "A man will leave his father and mother and be united with his wife, and the two will become one flesh."

Now, during this season of grieving, our kittens BB and CC seem to have devoted themselves to being my constant companions. Their meows for breakfast and purrs of appreciation and affection daily greet me in the early morning hours.

My breakfast prepared, I often sit in a comfortable chair positioned strategically in our living room picture window. There, I watch our cheerful and colorful feathered friends welcoming me to another day of life in this world. Here, too, I savor quiet, reflective time with my Jesus. Then I read Sara Young's devotional, *Jesus Calling*, some chapters in the One-Year Bible, and end the time with heartfelt prayer. A picture of Jack's animated, smiling face greets me as I walk down the hall. My morning is off to a glorious start.

Faithful Christian friends and neighbors continue to help fill my days of loneliness with love. I lean into gratitude, thanking God for all the answered prayers through the challenging and arduous journey we passed through with Parkinson's Disease, and I endeavor to remain grateful in this new stage, asking God to fill me with His peace, the one true peace that passes all understanding.

During this season, I often perceive that still, small voice of my Lord whispering in my ear. "Move on to my next career for you. I have something for you."

Do I think I know what it will be? Maybe. I invite you, my devoted family and faithful readers, to wait and see with me!

As Franklin Delano Roosevelt wrote in 1945, "The only limit to our realization of tomorrow will be our doubts of today. Let us move forward with strong and active faith. Let's take this journey together. Let us dream boldly and live fully."

Come with me as I continue to anticipate each new day's adventure of life on earth. And as I eagerly look forward to my greatest journey, a new life in heaven where I will reunite with beloved family and friends *and* see my Lord face-to-face. *That* will be the most incredible adventure of all!

Epilogue

Recently, in my writing class, our teacher Illia Thompson introduced the topic, "What is wealth?" She aimed to inspire our writing creativity. The word *wealth* brought a kaleidoscope of ideas sweeping through my mind. Pictures of the wealth and blessings I have experienced in my 86+ years of life swirl in vivid color in my head.

Henry David Thoreau wisely claimed, "Wealth is the ability to fully experience life." My loving Lord endowed me with that ability. I have enjoyed a rich, abundant life, arising largely through the tragic death of my father when I was four years old. That life-altering event planted a seed in my heart, one growing to become my life philosophy: "To look and live every moment of your life as if it were your last."

Viewing the tapestry of my life experiences, I acknowledge I am wealthy beyond my wildest imagination.

I reflect upon the humble but rich circumstances of my upbringing:

Frolicking freely through fresh-mowed alfalfa fields, inhaling their pungent aroma and listening to the birds singing a symphony just for me at four-and-a-half years old, living with my grandparents.

Benefitting from a range of inspiration and knowledge from my stepfather, a voracious reader, at eight years old. With his brilliant photographic mind, he seemed to retain all he read. He inspired me.

Swimming in the crashing waves of the Gulf of Mexico as well as the Officers' Club pool in Corpus, Christi, Texas, when Mother and I followed my stepfather, now a naval officer, to the Naval Air Station there. It was wartime; the Japanese had attacked Pearl Harbor. But I could enjoy the exhilaration and freedom of the sea!

Realizing my heart's desire – to experience a larger world – was starting to take shape as I gleaned rich life lessons from two new cultures – Texas and the U.S. military. Along with the latter, at nine, I began to gain a new understanding of the deep emotions of death when one of our neighbors, himself serving in the military, was killed in action.

And then, as I began to tiptoe into adulthood, yet more richness unfolded.

I delighted in being among some of the first women to complete bachelor's degrees in Post-WW II America. Only the thrill of learning superseded that distinction.

Then love literally knocked me off my feet. It wasn't long before I became Mrs. Howard Lincks, wed to a handsome, talented architect and gifted sportsman. In time our Lord blessed us with two darling daughters. And even with the tragedy of his early death due to cancer, God provided many silver linings.

For, in the spring of 1977, Jack Wulfmeyer entered our lives. The span of our marriage, over 41 years, allowed us to explore lands far and wide as well as share the love of Jesus Christ with thousands upon thousands of people via the Jesus Film Project.

Grandsons Spencer and Parker, now grown up, are among the treasures I cherish most.

And, even in the hard shadow of Parkinson's Disease, Jack and I experienced the blessings of walking hand-in-hand towards an eternity we'll experience together someday. Particularly meaningful was when we came together as a family and celebrated Jack's 90th birthday on September 9, 2019. And then, as I turned 86 a few months later on December 17th, Jack was able to wish me Happy Birthday three times – this just three days before he went to be with Jesus.

Now what? The holidays are past. The family has returned home. Here I am, a widow at 86 years old rattling around in an empty two-story house.

This particular winter has been unusually cold and wet. The dampness penetrates to my bones. The warmth of the fireplace soothes me as I respond with pen in hand to the outpouring of generosity and love in memory of Jack. My feathered friends at the bird feeder and my furry kittens attempt to fill my emptiness, not to mention my many family and friends.

I spend each morning reading my favorite devotional, *Jesus Calling*, by Sarah Young. I feel the outpouring of Christ's love and rich promises lavished upon me. He seems to be carrying me in his arms of comfort and peace.

My days are sometimes long. I am discovering my new life without caregiving. The release from a day filled with thinking every minute of Jack's needs is startling. Just walking out the front door without all my previous cares has made me feel as if I am floating without a tether. My first walk around the block without thinking to myself, "I must walk fast because I mustn't leave Jack very long" felt so strange after 10 years of caregiving.

In the earliest months following Jack's death, evenings proved to be especially lonely. Jack and I used to watch the news and then Jeopardy and Wheel of Fortune. But these activities only seem empty without him now. BB and CC, my cats, do keep me company, but the stillness sometimes grips me.

I soon discovered opening my computer and working on this book proved deeply fulfilling. I became so absorbed that some evenings the clock chiming at 11:00 pm shocked me.

My friend Caroline DePalatis has faithfully given her valuable time to help me edit this book. I will be forever grateful for her friendship, her commitment, and her encouragement. One of her other gifts was giving me the book *You Are A Writer, So Start Acting Like One*, by Jeff Goins. His book has inspired me to attend his fall conference for aspiring and published writers.

I've always said, "One can always have another career."

The world-famous artist Grandma Moses started painting at the age of 80. Am I going to be the Grandma Sue of writing, starting at 86? What a delightful thought!

Someday, when it's my turn to step into eternity, I will take great joy in reuniting with my mother and getting to know my father. I'll also be thrilled and surprised at the dear friends I will meet. Howard will welcome me, as will Jack and a plethora of family and friends I couldn't have even imagined.

In truth, all the worldly wealth put together cannot compare to walking down those streets of gold with Jesus for all eternity (Revelations 21).

I am ready. But I'm also taking great pleasure in these moments, days, weeks, months and years he has for me right now. That I may live them for His glory, right till the very end!

Appendix 1:
Mother Reflection

During my reading time recently, I discovered a short vignette authored by David Young entitled Mother's Day In Heaven. It inspired me to write this tribute to my mother.

Dedicated to my mother,
Carrie Elizabeth Jorgenson Gray Love

I can see her now, creating magic, the steady hum of her Singer sewing machine marking the moments as she depresses the pedal. I see her now sitting quietly with needle, thread and thimble by her bright light, deftly stitching and detailing the end of that fine seam.

There she is – the picture of a gifted fashion designer and exquisite seamstress, producing outfit after outfit from snow suits to formals, school clothes to cocktail dresses, and Easter and Christmas ensembles. Just for me.

Yes, I was always the best-dressed kid in grade school, often to my embarrassment. It wasn't until my teenaged years and beyond that I thoroughly appreciated and enjoyed the results of her talent and hard work. When granddaughters Jill and Holly were each born, my mother thrilled at arraying them in perfectly smocked dresses and coats with matching bonnets.

Burying herself in that talent, that activity, was

her little piece of heaven on this earth, helping her cope through all life's trials. During the last nine months of her life, as cancer sapped her body's strength, she lay piecing a lovely quilt by hand, stitch by stitch.

At age 64, on January 26, 1973, Carrie Elizabeth Jorgenson Gray Love's busy hands came to rest. Yet her gift of sewing lives on, especially in the quilts we all have been able to enjoy over many years since.

Eternally grateful, I look forward to the day I can say to her face to face, "Mother, there are so many things that happened throughout your life that I now understand."

There we stood, my elderly grandparents and me, at the front door of their home where my mother and I lived. They looked very awkward and in great discomfort. My five-year-old heart wondered why. At the same time I felt sad for them as they answered the knock at their front door. They knew they would open the door to Bob Ulm and cause him great pain.

For Bob was a widower who was squiring my mother. This old term for dating was used in the 1930s. He stood there with his five-year-old son, Wendell, squirming next to him. My grandfather nervously cleared his throat, took a deep breath and spoke with finality, "Carrie is not here."

In that era, not showing up for an appointed date translated into "I'm not interested in continuing our relationship." I saw his face fall as his eager anticipation suddenly turned into great despair.

Oh no! Oh no! I've hurt this sweet, gentle man!

These thoughts immediately raced through my head. I believed I was the one responsible for his crushed spirit. A huge wave of guilt washed over me.

Then a spark of anger flared up in my heart. I replayed the scene with my mother the previous night in my mind. Her question surprised me. "Would you like Wendell Ulm for a brother?" she inquired.

My immediate response was "No! That spoiled brat! He gets everything he wants and he's my same age, five years old." Now, I wondered who was the most spoiled after all.

A great swelling tide swept over me a few short years later. I felt like I was drowning. Trying to adjust to my new life with my stepfather, Martin Love, was a struggle.

During this time of transition, I believe my Mother came to realize she had met my questions about my father with complete silence. A silence of four long years. Suddenly, she felt compelled to acquaint me with my Father.

With deep sobs and many tears, she embarked on telling me about him. Her emotional outbursts confused me. I wondered, "Does she really love this man she is now married to?"

Now I realize she understood the potential influence a new father figure might have on my life. This led her to grapple with painful memories in order to acquaint me with my father. Thank you, Mother, for being willing to suffer in order to fill in some of the blanks in my life.

During my high school years, terrible fights would

erupt between my mother and stepfather. In the dark of night, the front door would slam and I would hear my mother sobbing.

I would steal myself as I lie in my bed just waiting for her pleading words, "Susie, Susie come to me."
I would never respond. I knew my stepfather could lose control of his temper very easily, and I didn't want to be his target. Forgive me Mother – my fear prevented me from reaching out to you in love and comfort.

Guilt and resentment stewed surreptitiously deep in my heart.

Ten years after her untimely death, I began to attend Bible Study Fellowship, or BSF as it is now known around the world. And it was through this process of studying God's Word I came face-to-face with my deep-seated judgmental attitude towards my mother.

As I grasped the depth and effect of my attitude, I instantly cried out in my spirit, "Oh, Mother, please forgive me. I am so sorry for not being a more loving, understanding and compassionate daughter. Forgive me for focusing on my feelings instead of reaching out to you in your pain."

My gifted, charming mother always tried to be the most loving mother she could be in spite of her tragedies and disappointments. I honestly was so ungrateful. Over and over again, in my spirit, I have begged her forgiveness and thanked her for being my devoted mother.

There's a perfect Mother's Day in heaven waiting for all of us with our mothers. It's the day I step from this eternal life into my life of glory. My spirit will wrap around her with a forever hug. We will be united and bonded as mother and daughter in pure love. There will be no sin to mar our togetherness. I can tell her how much I love her, how thankful I have been for her wealth of advice and say, "Mother, there aren't enough flowers in the whole wide world to thank you for the sweet fragrance of life you gave me."

Reunion day in heaven for me will fulfill all my heart's desires. Imagine it! I can picture it now. There's my Mother, Carrie. I will get to know my father, Robert. There will be my first love I was so crazy about, Howie, the father of my daughters.

And now, there will be my beloved Jack, my steady rock for so long, but mostly the best gift God gave me in my second season of life.

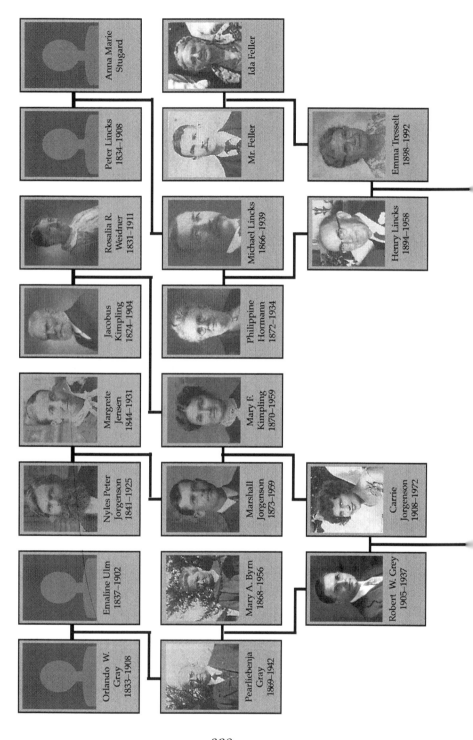

Anna Marie Stugard

Ida Feller

Peter Lincks 1834–1908

Mr. Feller

Emma Tresselt 1898–1992

Rosalia R. Weidner 1831–1911

Michael Lincks 1866–1939

Henry Lincks 1894–1958

Jacobus Kimpling 1824–1904

Philippine Hormann 1872–1934

Margrete Jensen 1844–1931

Mary F. Kimpling 1870–1959

Nyles Peter Jorgenson 1841–1925

Marshall Jorgenson 1873–1959

Carrie Jorgenson 1908–1972

Emaline Ulm 1837–1902

Mary A. Byrn 1868–1956

Robert W. Grey 1905–1937

Orlando W. Gray 1833–1908

Pearliebenja Gray 1869–1942

328

Appendix 2:
Gray~Lincks Family Tree

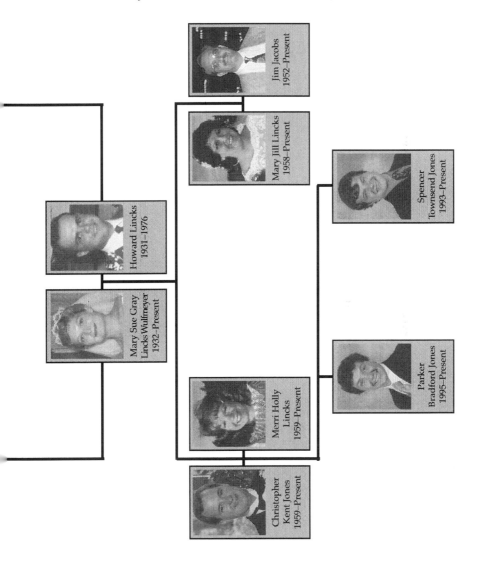

Jim Jacobs
1952–Present

Mary Jill Lincks
1958–Present

Howard Lincks
1931–1976

Mary Sue Gray
Lincks Wulfmeyer
1932–Present

Spencer
Townsend Jones
1993–Present

Parker
Bradford Jones
1995–Present

Merri Holly
Lincks
1959–Present

Christopher
Kent Jones
1959–Present

Appendix 3:
Memoir Acknowledgements

First, I want to thank my oldest daughter, Mary Jill Lincks Jacobs. She encouraged me to persist in writing about my life and the family genealogy. Next, I sing praises to my husband, Jack Allen Wulfmeyer. He scanned multiple pictures into my computer. He also patiently listened, edited, and endured my countless hours of midnight writing.

I am grateful to Illia Thompson, a former writing instructor at Monterey Peninsula College (MPC), for the discipline she required and the inspiration she gave me while attending her Memoirs Writing class. Thank you, Illia, for your training, the loving encouragement, and the tools to make this book possible.

Illia also introduced our class to Kathleen Sonntag, another instructor at MPC. Kathleen's computer expertise and her gift of organization proved invaluable for putting this book together.

A very special thanks to my cousin Arlene Chandler Whitaker for connecting me with unknown relatives.

It was a great thrill to learn for the first time of relatives Sandy and Nan Kimpling. Sandy sent me extensive records of her husband Paul Kimpling's family. Nan spent countless hours taping her family memories.

My cousin Carol Jane Chandler Bursott and her husband Richard Bursott spent their valuable time giving me newspaper clippings of family birth dates, marriages and deaths. They devoted an entire day taking me to three cemetaries to verify family dates. This proved especially valuable in searching for verification of the Gray family's geneology. We discovered a large bronze plaque at the Mount Pleasant Cemetary dating the Gray family history back to 1747. Many thanks to Stephen Lincks for supplying the geneology of the Lincks family dating back to 1702.

My eternal gratitude goes to Caroline DePalatis, a dear friend and author as well, who worked with me over the course of 1.5 years to edit my first draft and bring this book to completion. Her encouragement and support gave me great courage to persevere, especially during the difficult season of Jack's last stages of Parkinsons, his passage to Heaven and the season of grief and loss which has followed.

Caroline's husband Dale, a high school English instructor, as well as their amazing daughter, Erika, contributed significantly to this process as well, critiquing, further editing, and, in Erika's case, designing the layout of the book. Their family has been a true blessing to me.

Without each person's precious time and loving heart devoted to assisting me in this publication – as well as the encouragement of countless friends – *Roots & Petals* would not exist.

Words cannot express fully the abundant blessings and love I felt through this experience publishing my first book. Thank you one and all.

About the Author

Mary Sue Wulfmeyer is a mother and grandmother, mentor and friend to many. Since this is her personal memoir, there's not much extra to say except this is her first book. At 86, Lord wiling, Sue hopes to create more ahead!

If you enjoyed this book, please consider posting a review of it on Amazon.com. It is a great encouragement for a new author. If you purchased this book on Amazon, leave a review by going to "Orders," finding the book, then clicking on "Write a Review." If you did not purchase on Amazon, simply find the product by searching for the title then going to the review section and clicking the "Write a Review" button.

You can be in touch with Sue at
rootsandpetalsbook@gmail.com.

My Garden Blessing for You

I thank you for blessing my garden and continually watching over all that grows in it, making all things to flourish each in its season. And grant, O Lord, that all who come into my garden may know you personally and find the joy happiness, comfort and peace you have for each one of them.
Through Jesus Christ our Lord.

72972878R00209

Made in the USA
Columbia, SC
01 September 2019